Acknowledgments

Creating a book is never a solitary process involving only the author. My brother, Mike Butler, especially was a strong influence on my working on this book. His own excellent book, *Getting Around in Glacier National Park*, also published by America Through Time, set an example of excellence for me to try to achieve. He also provided insight into the publishing process and advice on how to proceed at many steps along the way.

Historic photos about the Civilian Conservation Corps in Glacier National Park featured in this book come from a wide range of sources. I have tried to be as specific as possible with the photo attributions and hope that I have done so accurately.

My thanks are extended to the good folks at America Through Time, the editorial and publishing team that worked with me in creating this book. It is a pleasure to work with such professionals.

Finally, thanks as always to my family for being willing to tolerate my ongoing obsession with Glacier National Park. This tolerance is very much appreciated.

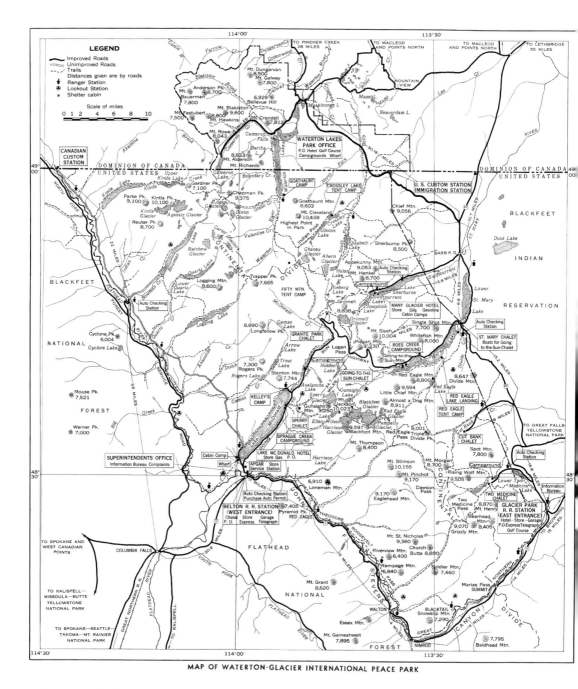

MAP OF WATERTON-GLACIER INTERNATIONAL PEACE PARK

Map of Glacier National Park during the CCC period, 1937. (*National Park Service*)

THE
CIVILIAN
CONSERVATION CORPS
IN
GLACIER NATIONAL PARK,
MONTONA

DAVID R. BUTLER

AMERICA
THROUGH TIME®
ADDING COLOR TO AMERICAN HISTORY

America Through Time is an imprint of Fonthill Media LLC
www.through-time.com
office@through-time.com

Published by Arcadia Publishing by arrangement with Fonthill Media LLC
For all general information, please contact Arcadia Publishing:
Telephone: 843-853-2070
Fax: 843-853-0044
E-mail: sales@arcadiapublishing.com
For customer service and orders:
Toll-Free 1-888-313-2665

www.arcadiapublishing.com

First published 2022

ISBN 978-1-63499-383-8

Typeset in 10pt on 13pt Sabon
Printed and bound in England

Contents

Introduction

In order to understand the history and significance of the Civilian Conservation Corps in Glacier National Park, we first need a basic understanding of the geography of the park. Glacier National Park was established in 1910 and is located in the Rocky Mountains of northwestern Montana, bordered on the north by easternmost British Columbia and westernmost Alberta, Canada; on the east by the Blackfeet Indian Reservation; on the south and southwest by Bear Creek and the Middle Fork of the Flathead River; and on the northwest by the North Fork of the Flathead River. The park is located astride the Continental Divide, which runs roughly northwest–southeast through the park. This divide basically subdivides the park into a moist, somewhat milder western half and a colder and drier eastern half.

Due to the moisture and temperature differences west and east of the Continental Divide, forests on the western side of the park are much taller, denser, and richer in a variety of tree species and understory vegetation. The forests of the east side are lower and more open, dominated by only a few species of trees, and give way to high plains grasslands near the eastern edge of the park and into the adjacent Blackfeet Reservation.

Local villages and other locations around and in Glacier Park have had an annoying tendency to change names over the course of park history. Park headquarters is on the west side of the park, immediately north of the Middle Fork of the Flathead River, adjacent to the modern village of West Glacier. West Glacier is also the western terminus of the world-famous Going-to-the-Sun Road that runs for 50 miles from West Glacier to St. Mary on the east border of the park. Try as you might, however, you will not find "West Glacier" on the 1930s-era park map shown here. Look instead for "Belton," the name of the Great Northern railroad station there. For the period of time of this book—1933–1942 when the Civilian Conservation Corps (hereafter in text "the CCC") operated in Glacier National Park—West Glacier did not exist. The village changed its name in 1949 to promote greater tourism. The railroad station there, however, remains known as Belton station, causing widespread confusion for train passengers wanting to disembark in West Glacier being told that they must get off in Belton.

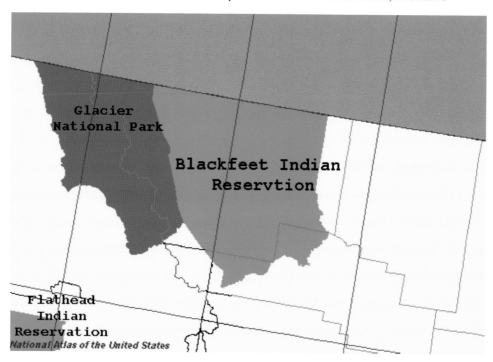

Map showing the position of Glacier National Park adjacent to the Blackfeet Nation/Indian Reservation to the east. Canada is the gray area to the north. (*National Atlas of the United States*)

A similar situation occurred on the east side of the park. Until the completion of the Going-to-the-Sun Road in 1933, a district headquarters for the east side of the park existed in the village of Glacier Park or Glacier Park Station, named for the Great Northern's Glacier Park railroad station. The village changed its name, also in 1949, to East Glacier Park (and known primarily simply as "East Glacier"). Nonetheless, like on the west side, the railroad station in East Glacier retains its original Great Northern "Glacier Park" name, causing east-side confusion for disembarking passengers as well.

In 1933, the east-side district headquarters for Glacier National Park was moved from Glacier Park Station (the future East Glacier) to St. Mary, in recognition that this eastern terminus of the new, completed Going-to-the-Sun Road would be a tourism growth center. Nearby, about 5 miles to the west on the road, is a campground and tourist facility known today as "Rising Sun", but known during CCC days as "Roes Creek" (which unfortunately was sometimes spelled as "Rose Creek," adding further to the place-name confusion). Going-to-the-Sun Road, running from west to east from Belton/West Glacier to St. Mary via Logan Pass, to this day remains the primary tourist attraction for the park.

U.S. Highway 2 and the tracks of the former Great Northern Railway, now the Burlington Northern and Santa Fe, parallel the southern boundary of the park between today's East Glacier and West Glacier. Two roads parallel the North Fork of the Flathead River on the park's northwestern side. One is the "outer road," which is a Forest Service road west of the river. The other is a somewhat awful gravel road, the Inside North Fork Road, that runs from the north shore of Lake McDonald at Fish Creek to the Kintla Lake turn-off (although the section north of the turn-off to Kintla Lake can be hiked to the site of the old Kishehnen ranger station). In spite of the bad quality of this road, numerous CCC activities took place along its margins.

The east side of Glacier Park has two primary, now paved, short tourist roads penetrating westward toward the mountains—the roughly 12 miles of the Many Glacier Road in the Swiftcurrent valley that traverses the north shore of Lake Sherburne, and the 7-mile-long Two Medicine Road about 5 miles north of East Glacier. A crude 5-mile-long gravel road penetrates the Cut Bank valley between Two Medicine and St. Mary to the north, and a few miles of the Chief Mountain highway cross the northeastern corner of the park.

With this "geography lesson" complete, let's move ahead into chapters that look at what the CCC was, the Glacier Park CCC camps, and what the CCC accomplished in the park between 1933 and 1942. We will finish with a look at the presidential trip of Franklin Roosevelt to Glacier National Park on behalf of the CCC in 1934.

1

The Civilian Conservation Corps

The Civilian Conservation Corps (CCC) was created by an act of Congress on March 30, 1933, through passage in both houses of Congress. The act was signed into law by President Franklin D. Roosevelt a day later. The CCC was the first economic relief program, and one of the main foundations, of Roosevelt's "New Deal" designed to bring America out of the depths of the Great Depression. It had been planned and proposed by Roosevelt, and subsequently passed in Congress, in less than a month after his inauguration as president on March 4, 1933—an amazingly quick span of time illustrating the seriousness of the economic emergency as viewed not only by the president but by both houses of Congress. The enabling legislation created an agency that was officially called the Emergency Conservation Work (ECW), but known across the country by the popular name that President Roosevelt gave it, the CCC. In 1937, the name was officially changed to the CCC to reflect this nationwide popular usage.[1,2]

By April 1933, young men, who were almost universally referred to as "CCC boys," were enrolling in this emergency employment program designed to provide jobs in aid of conservation activities to hundreds of thousands of young men. President Roosevelt's goal was to have 250,000 young men working by July 1.

> [The young men enrolled in the program would] work for the prevention of forest fires and for soil erosion, flood control, removal of undesirable plants, insect control, and construction or maintenance of paths, tracks, and fire lanes on public lands. In return, those enrolled in this program would be provided with appropriate clothing, daily subsistence, medical attention, hospitalization, and a cash allowance.... The Department of Labor was to initiate a nationwide recruiting program; the Army was to condition and transport enrollees to the work camps; and the Park Service and Forest Service were to operate the camps and supervise the work assignments.[3]

The Army's role was expanded when Park Service Director Horace Albright and Forest Service Chief Forester Robert Stuart realized that their agencies did not have enough men, equipment, or experience to operate the work camps 24 hours a day, so the Army was designated to operate and supervise the camps while the Park Service and Forest Service were to be responsible for the work projects.[4]

CCC boys were not subjected to military training or discipline, although the army ran the camps. Basically, the army simply transferred their organizational style and skills to CCC camps, using the same reports for morning reports, sick leave, and bookkeeping at camp post exchanges. Surplus army uniforms and fatigues were distributed, although non-army CCC-style buttons and insignias were designed and used (around 1937, new spruce green uniforms were designed and distributed to CCC workers to more clearly distinguish them from members of the army). CCC enrollees did not have to salute army officers, nor did they receive any combat-related training. Each CCC camp was designed, according to the wishes of President Roosevelt, to be comprised of approximately 200 men.[5, 6]

> Both the Forest Service and the Park Service opposed the 200-man quota because many of their jobs required fewer men. But they modified their programs to conform with presidential wishes. Another stipulation was that the bulk of the funds spent be on labor costs relating to work projects and not for the procurement of expensive equipment—that is, a bulldozer was not to be purchased, because there were enough men to do the same work.[7]

Enrollees were initially restricted to unmarried young men from eighteen to twenty-five years old who would agree to work for $30 per month and send $25 of their $30 wage check home to their families (in today's money, $30 per month translates to about $18 a day or a little over $2 an hour). As virtually all the young men who enrolled were unskilled, the rules were quickly changed on April 22 to allow for the hiring of a limited number of skilled men from the local areas around the CCC camps. These men were known as "locally employed men," or LEMs. Some LEMs became supervisors of the unskilled boys, as well as instructors in evening classes in the camps. With those greater responsibilities and skills, these fellows received the princely sum of $45 per month and became known as "$45 men". On May 11, veterans of World War I also became eligible to enroll in the CCC, although the number of those men was never more than a few thousand. They were also assigned to their own, more leniently run, camps, none of which existed in Glacier National Park.[8]

African-American young men were allowed to enroll in the CCC from its inception, but it quickly became apparent that the Jim Crow racial segregation that prevailed in the country at the time would be the norm in most CCC camps. Some CCC companies attempted to have integrated groups of white and black men working together, but in such cases, the whites would frequently either quit the program or ask for and receive a transfer to a different company, resulting in *de facto* segregated companies.

Native Americans were extended the right to enroll in the CCC on April 14, but because they worked on projects on their reservations, they did not need to live in camps but were allowed to go to their work projects in the day and return home at night. Few CCC-ID camps existed as a result, although as we will see at least

CCC men arrive at Missoula Station, 1933. CCC workers arrived by train in Missoula, Montana, and were subsequently distributed throughout northwest Montana for labor in the Flathead National Forest and Glacier National Park. (*K. D. Swan photo, U.S. Forest Service*)

Above left: CCC uniforms were U.S. Army surplus and so looked like army fatigues except for the various CCC insignias, including this collar button. (*Photo from Creative Commons*)

Above right: Typical shoulder patch for a CCC-ID unit, in this case for the Uintah and Ouray Agency. (*Records of the Bureau of Indian Affairs, RG 75*)

two CCC-ID camps existed for unspecified periods on the Blackfeet Reservation immediately adjacent to Glacier Park. The Native American enrollees were also overseen by a separate administrative structure, called the CCC-Indian Division, known casually as the CCC-ID. The CCC-ID assigned work projects separately from the CCC, with projects chosen by reservation superintendents.[9]

CCC enrollees initially received training, conditioning, and housing on army bases across the country. Fort Missoula, Montana—a "sleepy relic of the 1877 Nez Perce Indian uprising situated on the edge of Missoula, Montana"—served as the training and dispersal point for CCC boys who would be assigned to camps in national forests and national parks throughout the northern intermountain region, including in both Yellowstone and Glacier National Parks.[10]

2

Glacier Park's CCC Camps

CCC workers began arriving in Glacier National Park in the late spring and summer of 1933.

> Never before and never again was so large and steady a stream of labor to flow into Glacier. That the national parks became focal points for indirect stimulation of the economy through the activities of the CCC was no coincidence. Franklin Roosevelt gave executive support to his strong personal conviction that the national parks be identified as "pump-priming agencies."[1]

All the camps and companies in the park were under the administration of the Fort Missoula CCC region. The camps were organized and run by U.S. Army personnel, but the projects chosen and the work assignments were decided upon and administered by the superintendent of Glacier National Park, as advised by Glacier National Park staff. The superintendent and staff were responsible for inspection of the work done, overseeing camp superintendents, and keeping them on appropriate work schedules. These staff members were primarily from the park's already overworked park rangers, so the importance of LEMs in advising on and directing projects in the field became quickly apparent. The Fort Missoula CCC district also oversaw the administration of CCC-Indian Division (CCC-ID) camps, including on the Blackfeet Reservation bounding Glacier Park to the east, although the Army ran the CCC campsites and companies of workers. The superintendent of the Blackfeet Reservation recruited the Blackfeet enrollees and planned the work projects.

CCC workers assigned by Fort Missoula to camps in Glacier National Park arrived, after orientation and training at army bases including at Fort Missoula itself for a minority of the workers, via the Great Northern Railway at Belton Station in Belton (West Glacier) for the west side camps. Workers assigned to the east side camps in the park disembarked at Glacier Park Station (now East Glacier Park). CCC-ID workers came from local residents of the Blackfeet Reservation.[2]

Belton Station in what is now West Glacier, the first stop for CCC boys after training at Fort Missoula in Missoula. Workers at Park west-side camps disembarked here; workers destined for east-side camps continued on to Glacier Park Station in what is now East Glacier. (*Fred H. Kiser photo, Oregon Historical Society Library ba021214*)

View of Belton Station, the village of Belton, and the Belton Hills as it would have looked to CCC boys coming in on the train from training at Fort Missoula. (*R. E. Marble photo, Glacier National Park GLAC 6104*)

View of Belton Station in West Glacier, looking eastward. (*Photo by author, July 23, 2012*)

Above: View of Belton Station and the Belton Hills draped in clouds behind the station, looking eastward from across U.S. Highway 2. (*Photo by author, July 5, 1988*)

Below: Westbound Empire Builder passenger train at Glacier Park Station, June 10, 1934, view looking northeastward. Glacier Park Station was the disembarkation point for CCC boys going to east-side camps. (*George A. Grant photo, GNP GLAC 11489*)

Modern view of Glacier Park Station, also looking northeast-bound. (*Photo by author, July 21, 2012*)

Westward-looking view of Glacier Park Station. (*Photo by author, July 21, 2012*)

Eight CCC camps were established in Glacier Park in 1933, five on the west side and three on the east side of the park. Each camp held approximately 200 CCC boys. Only one camp, Camp GNP-1 at McDonald Creek on the west side, was comprised of CCC boys from Montana. The other seven CCC camps were populated with workers from New York (six camps) and Pennsylvania (one camp). Also on the west side of the park, Camp GNP-2 was located at Apgar, and its workers were from Fort Hamilton, New York. Camp GNP-3, located at Fish Creek at the southern end of the Inside North Fork Road, had workers from Fort Niagara, New York. Although Camp GNP-8, located along the Inside North Fork Road at Anaconda Creek, was originally meant to be an integrated camp, complaints and subsequent transfers from white CCC workers resulted in a segregated so-called "Negro Camp" of African-American young men from Brooklyn, New York. Camp GNP-9 was the Pennsylvania contingent, located in Belton adjacent to the Middle Fork of the Flathead River. This distribution of camps was designed primarily to provide for work to be done around Park headquarters, in the large area between Belton and Apgar burned in a massive forest fire in 1929, along the Going-to-the-Sun Road west of Logan Pass, and along the Inside North Fork Road and at ranger stations along that road.[3]

Most Glacier Park CCC Camps were comprised of tents only. Permanent structures were built in the camps in Belton and at Apgar Flats near Lake McDonald. Due to the temporary tent-structure nature of most park camps, only the camps with permanent structures on the west side of the park were kept open during the harsh Glacier Park winters. The permanent camps with winter CCC workers had frame bunk houses, a mess hall, a radio room, and a library. Workers in the temporary camps were assigned to other camps elsewhere, in other states with warmer climates, over the winter months.[4]

One of the criticisms of the 200-man camps was that they were not sufficiently flexible to accommodate work projects, such as constructing fire trails connecting west-side valleys adjacent to the Inside North Fork Road, that demanded fewer men but were far from camp and/or away from roads in the extensive park backcountry. The solution for this problem was the establishment of so-called "spike camps," small side camps typically holding roughly twenty to fifty enrollees. One such camp, for example, was established at Bowman Lake with fifty-two workers from Camp GNP-8 on Anaconda Creek. Other spike camps included Walton, Nyack, Anaconda Creek (presumably a different location on the creek than Camp GNP-8), and Round Prairie on the west side of the park, at Logan Pass, and at Roes Creek and Cut Bank on the east side.[5, 6, 7]

On the east side of the park, camps were established in 1933 near Many Glacier at the head of Lake Sherburne (Camp GNP-4) with workers from New York City, along the north shore of Lake Sherburne at No Name Creek (Camp GNP-5) with workers from New York and New Jersey, and on Lower Two Medicine Lake in the southeastern part of the park near Glacier Park (East Glacier) (Camp GNP-6) with workers from New York. Notice that for whatever reason, there was no "GNP-7" camp in the 1933 numbering system.

The year 1934 saw the same number of CCC camps in the park, all but one of which were the same as in 1933. Camp GNP-2, at Apgar, was not re-established in

Former site of CCC Camp GNP-8, Anaconda Creek, along the Inside North Fork Road on the western side of Glacier National Park. (*Photo by author, July 26, 1994*)

Glacier National Park CCC Camp GNP-2 near present-day Apgar. (*George A. Grant photo, GNP*)

View from Apgar, *c.* 1909, looking up Lake McDonald, near future site of CCC Camp GNP-2. (*Fred H. Kiser photo, Oregon Historical Library ba020963*)

CCC Camp GNP-15, "Apgar Flats," was to become one of the primary park installations. It is shown here in 1934, before the construction of winter barracks. (*Glacier National Park*)

CCC Camp GNP-3, Fish Creek Camp, along the Inside North Fork Road (the light-colored scar running across the left-center of the photo). The forested area shown was extensively burned in 1926. (*Glacier Natural History Association*)

CCC living quarters at Fish Creek Camp, Apgar Range in the background, 1936. (*Chris Fitzgerald and "Building America—The CCC"*)

A "spike camp" at Bowman Lake that served fifty-two workers from the Anaconda Creek GNP-8 camp. (*Glacier National Park Annual Report, 1934*)

1934. A new Camp GNP-11, at Roes/Rose Creek at the present-day location of the Rising Sun Camp Store and Motor Inn on the north shore of St. Mary Lake (and sometimes referred to as the "St. Mary Camp"), added to the workforce on the east side of the park.

Subsequent years saw some of the original camps being closed and new camps being opened. After about 1935, fewer camps per year were typical, with four camps typifying the period 1940-1942. For example, on July 1, 1935, seven camps were on duty, four on the east side, and three on the west. They remained until October, when the workers from six camps were moved to warmer camps elsewhere, and only Camp GNP-1 remained occupied over the winter.

Additional camps were eventually established at Belton and Apgar Flats on the west side (CCC Camps GNP-12 and GNP-15, respectively), and a new, different camp on Lake Sherburne on the east side (CCC Camp GNP-13). In May and June 1936, three camps were occupied in addition to Camp GNP-1 that over-wintered—Camps GNP-13, GNP-3, and GNP-9, listed in chronological order of their occupancy for a total of only four camps over the summer of 1936. Once again, the numbering system escapes logic, as there were apparently never any camps numbered GNP-10 nor GNP-14. This distribution of workers allowed for maintenance work and vegetation clearing by workers along Going-to-the-Sun Road, continued clearing of burned forest between Belton and Apgar, maintenance of the Many Glacier Road, and keeping the Lake Sherburne reservoir clean and clear of debris.[8, 9]

By 1937, the number of CCC Camps in the park seems to have stabilized at four. In 1938 and 1939, two camps each were on the west and the east sides during summer. Over the winter of 1938, three camps remained operative in the Belton–Apgar area. The same pattern characterized 1938 and 1939, 1939–1940, and 1940–1941. During

Aerial view of Lake Sherburne and dam. CCC Camp GNP-5 was located along the lake at left-center above the lake. (*Photo by author, August 9, 1995*)

Group photo, looking westward toward Grinnell and Salamandar Glaciers at lower left center, of CCC Camp GNP-5, Company 281, September 29, 1934. (*Glacier National Park Annual Report, 1934*)

Group photo at a different angle, CCC Camp GNP-5, Company 281, looking toward Appekunny Mountain. (*Glacier National Park Annual Report, 1934*)

Near the head of Lake Sherburne, looking up valley, the site of CCC Camp GNP-5 barely visible on the right, 1941. (*Marion Post Walcott photo, Library of Congress*)

Looking southward across the headwaters of Lake Sherburne, to the site of CCC Camp GNP-4, Many Glacier, on the flat, open areas at lower center. (*Photo by author, August 20, 1991*)

Hand-colored photo of the site that would become CCC Camp GNP-4, looking toward Altyn Peak, *c.* 1910. (*Fred H. Kiser photo, Oregon Historical Society Library ba021188*)

Packing up for loading on a pack train, *c.* 1910, at the future site of CCC Camp GNP-4, Altyn Peak in the rear. (*Fred H. Hiser photo, Oregon Historical Society Library ba021190*)

CCC Camp GNP-4, looking toward Altyn Peak, July 4, 1933. (*George A. Grant photo, National Park Service*)

Closer view of the boys of CCC Camp GNP-4, posing at lunchtime. (*George A. Grant photo, Glacier National Park GLAC 11487*)

Group of young men at CCC Camp GNP-4 at Many Glacier, made up mostly of boys from New York City, July 3, 1933. In the center is Dominick Laulette, said to be the shortest man in the CCC "Army". (*George A. Grant photo, public domain, Wikipedia Commons*)

July 1942, all CCC activities in the park were abandoned and terminated when nationally the CCC was terminated as a funded program. By its end, nearly 11,500 CCC enrollees had served in Glacier National Park.[10, 11]

Little information exists on the number of CCC-ID Camps on the Blackfeet Reservation on the eastern border of Glacier National Park. One reason for this is that, unlike the CCC camps, CCC-ID workers had the option of working out of their homes if the work was within a reasonable distance. Many of the Blackfeet CCC-ID workers lived in East Glacier, Babb, or the tribal headquarters in Browning and could reach work along the Glacier Park border in short order, so it was simply not necessary to create a large number of CCC-ID Camps next to the park. Two that did exist were located at Lower Two Medicine Lake, and at the base of Divide Mountain. The Lower Two Medicine Lake camp cooperated with Glacier Park CCC workers in keeping Lower Two Medicine Lake clear of floating debris and material that could clog the dam intake. The camp at the base of Divide Mountain was in telephone communication with the Divide Mountain Indian Service Lookout on the mountain ridge above, and workers at this camp were prepared to be dispatched for fire suppression at any time. Both the Lookout and the CCC-ID camp at Divide Mountain were also in direct telephone communication with the National Park Service in Glacier National Park. A reference exists to "the Indian CCC up at the Many Glacier and Swift Current camps," but no other information exists about this or these camps, and documentation to the contrary shows that the enrollees at Camps GNP-4 and GNP-5 were from New York and New Jersey. In addition, no word of an adjacent CCC-ID camp is mentioned in any of the surviving camp newspapers from the CCC camps at Many Glacier and Lake Sherburne.[12, 13]

Location of one of the Blackfeet CCC-ID camps beneath the Divide Mountain Lookout (small structure on mountain ridge "bump" just left of center) on the Glacier National Park/Blackfeet Reservation boundary. The fire watcher in the lookout communicated with the CCC-ID camp via a surface phone line installed by workers of the CCC-ID. (*Photo by author, July 20, 2012*)

3

Life in the Camps

What was life like in the CCC Camps of Glacier National Park? Each camp had roughly 200 CCC boys, as well as three to five army staff officers running the camps and six to eight National Park Service work project staff. As previously noted, the army ran the camps but had nothing to do with work assignments or projects. The Park Service staff oversaw the work in each camp, and the park superintendent and his staff doled out the projects to be carried out by each camp.

> A supervisor, who was also provided for each project, worked with and directed several CCC foremen. Army personnel, meanwhile, had authority for general company supervision and welfare during hours not spent in actual work. Civilian project supervisors within each company divided work parties into sections and sub-sections, each led by technicians and sub-alterns.[1]
>
> Medical care was provided for the men. Each camp was assigned a physician who was possibly a regular army man or a reservist called to CCC duty, or more usually, a civilian hired under contract by the district medical officer. Frequently the doctors spent only part of their time on CCC work and had their own practice in a nearby town.... Whenever possible, one doctor served two or three main camps as well as any side camps in the area.[2]

Camp life was not subject to military discipline, but the daily schedules were laid out by the army with military precision. A typical day began at 6 a.m. with a bugle sounding reveille or a whistle announcing "first call."

> The enrollees arose, washed, dressed, and straightened the barracks, under the supervision of the barracks leader and his assistant. Then the boys went to the mess hall for breakfast, served an hour after reveille. After the meal they assembled at 7:45 a.m. for roll call and physical training, conducted by the camp commander. At 8:00 a.m. the enrollees left for the work project. If they were near camp, the boys walked back for dinner at 12:00 noon. If not, they ate a field lunch, sometimes a hot meal

but usually consisting of sandwiches, coffee, and fruit. The men reassembled at 12:45 to resume work. At 4:00 p.m. they returned to camp, cleaned up and put on their dress uniforms with black tie. After supper, which was served at 5:30 p.m., the men could enjoy some recreation.[3]

CCC boys worked forty-hour weeks and had weekends off unless a forest fire required their attention on weekends.

Of the original eight CCC camps in the park, each had eight to twenty LEMs recruited from the surrounding communities. Initially, local communities were concerned about the importation of "outsiders," especially from the east coast, into conservative northwest Montana. However, the use of local labor as LEMs helped bring about acceptance of the CCC camps by the local communities affected by their presence. The LEMs were also a steadying influence for the CCC boys from the east, almost all of whom were strangers to being out in nature and the woods.[4, 5]

The bulk of Glacier Park's camps were temporary camps, with permanent camps only in and near Belton on the park's west side. Temporary camps did have some wooden buildings, typically an oil house (service station), generator house, bath house, latrine, and mess hall. A garage/vehicle maintenance building was built for some as well. CCC boys lived in army surplus tents in the temporary camps. A standard camp had forty-six army tents with wood frames and floors, with thirty-four such tents serving as barracks for the CCC boys and the other tents given over for army offices and quarters, a supply tent, an infirmary, and larger education and recreation tents. Barracks, typically four, were built in the permanent camps along with a headquarters and living quarters for the army personnel overseeing the camps, mess hall, bath house, education building, recreation building, latrines, and a water pump house.[6]

Daily Life in the Camps

With only a minimal army presence in camps in terms of the number of personnel, many of the day-to-day aspects of life fell to the CCC boys themselves. Without the benefits of such conveniences as an army barber or army-run laundry, enrollees became of necessity involved with providing haircuts for buddies, doing their own laundry, and other self-care tasks.

The quality and quantity of food in the camps of Glacier Park varied by location. Overall, the army did a good job of supplying food to the camps, and a typical CCC boy in the park from Brooklyn wrote "[m]y muscles are hard as iron and I have gained fifteen pounds in weight." Nonetheless, one camp in particular, Camp GNP-15, had more problems with food quality and quantity than the others. That camp was notorious for lousy and small breakfasts and overall bad quality food. One CCC boy, Nelson Spaulding from Alexander, New York, remembered a song that was popular among the enrollees with whom he served during his time in Glacier Park:

Left: "Barbershop" in operation at CCC Camp GNP-2 in Apgar, at the foot of Lake McDonald. (*Photo by George A. Grant, National Park Service*)

Below: Washing and drying clothes, CCC Camp GNP-2 in Apgar. (*National Park Service photo HPC-000575*)

In Glacier National Park
The home of the fleas
The home of the bed bugs
And the CCC's
We sing loudest praises
And boast of its fame
While starving to death
On this government plain
How happy we are,
When the cooks go to bed
We hope in the morning
We find them all dead.[7]

Another "song" denoting the monotony of meals was "Beans yesterday, beans today, more beans for a rainy day." Food at Camp GNP-15 was sufficiently bad over the course of 1940–1941 that one of the LEMs told the army camp commander that he was refusing to take his boys out to work after a breakfast of "black coffee, burnt toast, and wormy oatmeal." An hour later, they were given some bacon and eggs and agreed to report for work, but the poor food continued over the following week.

The situation came to boil at an evening meal when the CCC boys marched in and staged a food strike. "Plates were filled and someone whistled. They all lined up to the garbage cans with their filled plates and dumped them without anyone taking a bite." A subsequent investigation revealed massive embezzling of food by an army sergeant in collaboration with the camp commander. Among other things, six tons of sugar and two tons of potatoes were "re-directed" to a small store for re-sale in a nearby town.[8, 9]

Camp mascots were common across the Glacier Park CCC camps, but not perhaps what you might think of as "normal" or "usual" mascots. Stray dogs were, of course, favorites that were immediately adopted. Wandering black bear cubs were also a favorite. CCC boys at Lake Sherburne on the east side captured and kept a beaver that they fed with carrots, until forced by the supervisors to turn it loose. Perhaps the most unusual was a moose calf, adopted in the spring of 1934 at Camp GNP-8 at Anaconda Creek. It was found along the Inside North Fork Road on the first day in camp that year. Although the army officers and work foreman immediately had it returned to where it was found, the baby moose returned the following day and took up a position in front of the kitchen door. It finally wandered off on its own after a few days of hanging around the camp. Camp GNP-8 also adopted a Franklin grouse nesting in the middle of camp that was reportedly "well fed."[10, 11]

Camp GNP-8 had a reputation for being somewhat eccentric, and that reputation deserves scrutiny. In 1934, the camp held the "national title" in the CCC for most cigarettes sold in the camp PX, and the PX steward reported selling 40,000 to 50,000 cigarettes monthly. He also reported selling 8,000 candy bars per month. One must therefore inquire why this camp sold so many cigarettes and candy bars. Recall that Camp GNP-8 was the *de facto* segregated camp at Anaconda Creek, many miles north of Belton on the Inside North Fork Road. The sad fact is that the enrollees bought their cigarettes and candy bars in camp because they were not welcomed by the merchants of Belton. Shopkeepers there posted "We cater to white trade only" signs in their stores and were reportedly "prejudiced against enrollees because of their race". This led to a high desertion rate in Camp GNP-8 such that by October, 1934, only sixty-four black enrollees remained (recall that the park camps had a normal average of about 200 enrollees).[12, 13]

Religious services were typically provided by religious leaders from surrounding towns. Trips into Whitefish or Kalispell for CCC boys on the west side of the park were also feasible. CCC boys on the east side could attend services in Babb or East Glacier Park.

Recreation during evenings and especially weekends was highly prized by the CCC boys, covering a range of activities ranging from organized intramural-stye baseball teams, to boxing matches, pitching horseshoes, volleyball, ping-pong games, and shooting competitions. Swimming was a favorite pastime in the cold mountain lakes at Lake McDonald and Lake Sherburne, as was fishing in those lakes as well as St. Mary Lake and lakes in the Two Medicine valley. Evening movies were also popular across the various park camps. Occasional dances, with bands and female company from the surrounding towns, were also very popular. "Camp Night" was also a popular activity, being essentially a combination talent show and sing-along for the CCC boys.[14, 15]

This photo was presented by President Franklin D. Roosevelt to King George VI of England. It shows CCC boys diving into Lake McDonald near Apgar, in Glacier National Park. (*U.S. Government Printing Office*)

Educational Resources and Activities

Educational lectures and "field trips" (basically day hikes from camps, sometimes with a ranger-naturalist guide) were also popular activities, with lectures in the evenings and field trip hikes on weekends. Hikes to Grinnell Glacier and Iceberg Lake were popular destinations for the CCC boys in the Swiftcurrent valley on the east side. The annual Babb Rodeo on the east side of the park was a popular spectator activity, as were trips to Cardston, Alberta. West-side trips into Kalispell or Whitefish for shopping and socializing were also popular.[16]

Evening educational lectures covered a range of topics. One of the most popular speakers was Francis X. "Frank" Guardipee, the only Blackfeet park ranger at that time in Glacier Park. Guardipee was a well-known local figure, who often served as a liaison between the Park Service and the Blackfeet tribal elders. His lectures were given on both sides of the park, in Belton and in the Swiftcurrent valley. His usual approach was educating the all-white CCC crowd about the Blackfeet tribe, using a combination of historical information, demonstrations, and humorous interactions with the audience.[17, 18]

Organized educational classes were also a mainstay of evenings in the CCC camps, covering a broad range of topics. Some classes were designed for vocational training, whereas others covered academic topics. Many CCC boys were able to earn the equivalent of a high school diploma through attendance in camp classes combined with correspondence courses.

Classes offered in the Glacier Park CCC camps varied, of course, by camp. Information on which courses characterized which camps comes from the various camp newspapers that have survived until today. Unfortunately, no copies of camp newspapers from Two Medicine, Rising Sun/St. Mary, Anaconda Creek, or Apgar survive (although individual copies may reside in family collections, and if any readers have such copies, they are encouraged to contact the author). Fortunately, copies survive in varying number from park CCC camps in Belton, and the Swiftcurrent valley, and the following extracts of course offerings are taken primarily from those newspapers along with independent historical accounts.

Vocational classes taught skills that would allow CCC boys to find employment quickly when their enrollment period was up, and were very popular. As many of Glacier Park's CCC enrollees were from New York City and surrounding urban areas, many of them did not know how to drive. Driving classes were, therefore, very popular, and upon completion, some of the better drivers were assigned to drive trucks in the camps. Driving was taught at Camp GNP-13, at Lake Sherburne, and elsewhere. Classes there were also taught in how to be an auto mechanic and surveying. Additional classes at Camps GNP-4 and GNP-13 included radio operations, photography, woodcarving, first aid, dark room (photography), typing, and psychology. Classes in the camps in and near Belton were similar.[19]

Correspondence courses were also popular in camps on both sides of the park. These courses were designed more for assisting the CCC boys to achieve their eighth grade or high school diploma equivalent, although some also taught vocational-tech material. Also available were university correspondence courses for college credit.

Left: Lectures by National Park Service rangers were frequently given for educational purposes to the Park CCC camps. Francis X. (Frank) Guardipee, shown here in 1945, was the only Blackfeet park ranger during this period and was a popular lecturer for the CCC. (*National Park Service*)

Below: Frank Guardipee—shown here with his wife Alma, son Gunner, and family dog—gave lectures to CCC camps on both sides of the park, at Belton as well as to the combined Many Glacier/Lake Sherburne camps. His topic was typically on the Blackfeet Nation. (*Glacier National Park archives*)

Courses available included auto mechanics, blueprint reading, business English, diesel engine mechanics, forestry, journalism, photography, psychology, business law, mental hygiene, pen lettering/calligraphy, and typewriting.[20]

Camp Newspapers

Many of the park's CCC camps published camp newspapers that were issued on an irregular basis. As they were mimeographed and distributed to camp members, very few examples survive to today, and it is simply not known if camp newspapers were produced in the camps at Two Medicine, Rising Sun/St. Mary, Apgar, or Fish Creek. The name of the paper from Camp GNP-8 at Anaconda Creek is known and speaks volumes about the situation faced by the African-American enrollees there—the paper was called *Isolation*. Unfortunately, no examples of this paper survive to my knowledge. Examples of camp newspapers that have survived include the *Belton Beacon* from 1936 (the specific Belton-area camp(s) covered by this paper were not identified), the *Glacier Ice Sheet* from 1935 for Camps GNP-4 and GNP-13 in the Swiftcurrent valley, the *Babb Gazette* from 1936 from the same area, and the *Babb Echo*, which was a continuation of the *Babb Gazette*.[21]

The park camp papers all had a similar format. They included news of the army officers of the camp and their comings and goings, reports on the arrival of new recruits and well-wishes for departing CCC boys whose enrollment period was up, jokes about the food, reports on social activities such as the dances and camp nights, scores and reports on camp baseball games held against other park camps or teams from Cardston (Alberta), reports on other sports including discussion about fishing, jokes, song lyrics and music for camp sing-a-longs, camp gossips (including good-natured "ribbing" about which CCC boy was seeing a "local" girl or hotel employee), information about religious services, and information on the camp classes and educational opportunities. Some of the papers described recent field trips to surrounding communities or to scenic sites in the park.

An additional feature common to the papers were amusing cartoons commenting on camp life, drawn by a talented cartoonist-member of the newspaper staff. These cartoons ranged from topics about sports, to kitchen work (KP), to poking fun at individual camp members who had done something "notable." Nicknames rather than full names of the individuals poked fun at were used, but it is very likely that everyone reading the camp paper would know the individual in question.

CCC-ID camps were not common because the Native Americans could often return home each evening, but some reservations did have camps such as those described for the Blackfeet Reservation. A photo of the cover of *Tom Tom Echoes*, from the Blackfeet Reservation and specifically noted from tribal headquarters in Browning, Montana, survives, but no known copies of the text of the newspaper could be located. It is also unknown if this paper served to cover news from one specific camp on the reservation or represented an amalgam of information gathered from all the reservation camps including those along the Glacier Park boundary described in Chapter 2.

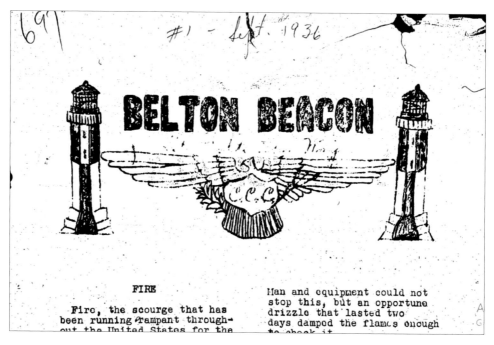

Front page of the camp newspaper for the CCC camp in Belton (West Glacier), September 1936. (*Center for Research Libraries*)

Above left: The front cover of an issue of the *Glacier Ice Sheet*, the combined camp newspaper for CCC Camps GNP-4 and GNP-5 near Many Glacier in the Swiftcurrent valley. (*Center for Research Libraries*)

Above right: The final *Glacier Ice Sheet* front cover, from the September 15, 1935, issue. Note the "G.N.P. Farewell" hanging sign. (*Center for Research Libraries*)

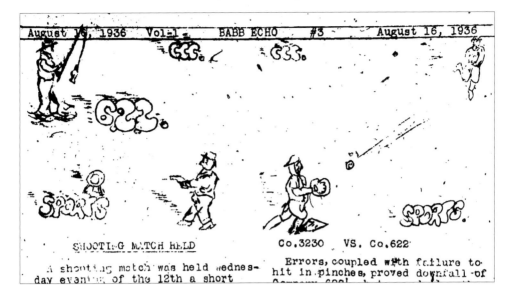

Sports were a favorite topic in all the Park CCC camp newspapers. This cartoon illustrates fishing, target shooting, and baseball, and is from the August 16, 1936, issue of the *Babb Echo*. (*Center for Research Libraries*)

Amateur cartoonists were a staple of the Park CCC camp newspapers. This cartoon, from the August 16, 1936, issue of the *Babb Echo*, shows one of the National Park rangers bringing freshly caught fish back to "Happy Cookie" at the Mess building. (*Center for Research Libraries*)

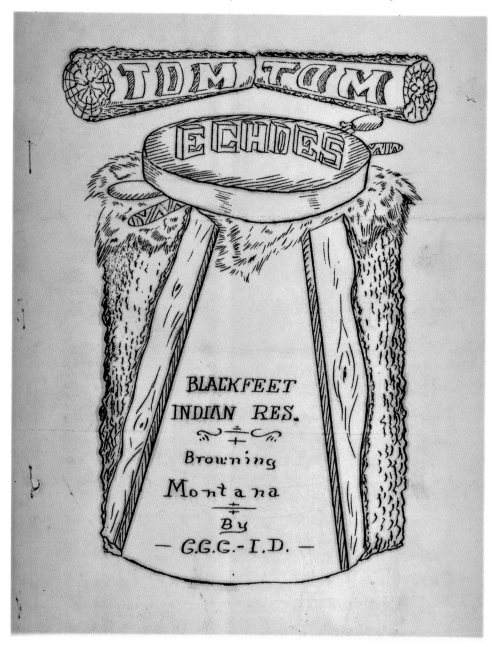

The CCC-ID camps also had newspapers, as illustrated here for the undated *Tom Tom Echoes* from the Blackfeet Reservation. (*Records of the Bureau of Indian Affairs, RG75*)

4

Firefighting by the CCC in Glacier National Park

From its creation in 1933, one of the primary purposes of the CCC in the western United States was to fight forest fires. In Glacier National Park, specific squads of firefighting specialists known as "flying squads" were created in each CCC camp to assist the park's firefighting crews when necessary. Camp supervisors, using rangers as instructors, organized the flying squads, which were well-equipped and mobile crews of fifteen to thirty men who were subject to immediate call during the fire season. Each park CCC camp had a "fully equipped light truck ready for instant response in case of fire. This first crew was backed up by a 100-man squad in case the fire could not be contained by the flying squads." In 1936, the park expanded the fire training to include every CCC enrollee, while still maintaining the flying squads. The flying squads were sent first to a fire, but if a fire could not be suppressed, then the full number of camp enrollees could be called in.[1]

Glacier Park's CCC camps were heavily involved in fighting forest fires from the arrival of the enrollees in 1933. In that first year alone, which was a dry summer with numerous fires, camp GNP-1 spent 15,780 man-hours fighting forest fires, 4,800 man-hours were spent at camp GNP-2, 8,784 man-hours from camp GNP-3, 25,560 man-hours from camp GNP-4, 25,416 man-days from camp GNP-5 (note the different measure versus man-hours), 14,880 man-hours from camp GNP-6 at Two Medicine, 7,224 man-hours from camp GNP-8, and 6,840 man-hours from camp GNP-9.[2]

During the ten years of the CCC's existence from 1933 to 1942, some years in Glacier Park were very quiet and some were very busy in terms of the number of forest fires needing to be fought by CCC boys. The year 1933, as mentioned above, was very busy. The next major fire year was 1936, described in more detail in a subsequent section, and 1940 was noted as follows:

> One of the worst fire seasons in the history of the Park and the CCC proved to be invaluable in prompt, effective action on a large number of fires. Had not trained and organized CCC crews been available it is certain that many thousands of acres of forested area would have burned.[3]

CCC boys were instrumental in reducing the amount of park acreage burned by forest fires each summer, also helping to prevent large fires such as the Heavens Peak fire of 1936 from increasing the amount of acreage burned. By 1940, CCC workers on both sides of the park had contributed nearly 84,000 man-days to forest fire suppression and prevention. The nature of the 1940 fire season can be seen in the annual superintendent's report for that summer, where it was noted that "(a) total of 106,269 CCC man-hours were spent in the suppression of reportable fires." Many of those 1940 fires were in difficult-to-reach locations east of the Middle Fork of the Flathead River and U.S. Highway 2 or east of the Inside North Fork Road between Fish Creek and Bowman Lake.[4]

Reconstructing where CCC boys were deployed to fight fires in Glacier Park is frustratingly difficult. For the park superintendent reports from 1933 to 1942, only the final report from 1942 provides details on the specific fires of that year. Unfortunately, in that single case, although acreage of area burned is provided, no information was given about which fires were fought by the CCC. The superintendent did note for the fire season of 1940 that nearly all fires in that bad season were fought by CCC boys, and given the chronic manpower shortage in the National Park Service ranks in the park, it is logical to assume that most fires were primarily fought by the CCC under Park Service direction.[5, 6]

The Heaven's Peak Fire of 1936

The most notable fire fought by the CCC in Glacier Park was the Heaven's Peak Fire of 1936, notable for both its size and because it burned through some of the most accessible, tourist-visited sections of the park. The fire burned a large swath across the McDonald Creek valley, up the west side of the Garden Wall, progressed over Swiftcurrent Pass and onto the east side of the park, and down the popular Swiftcurrent valley. Before it was finally vanquished, the fire burned over 7,600 acres in the heart of the park.[7]

The fire began with a lightning strike on August 18, on a very steep slope on the flank of Heaven's Peak, the large mountain that towers above McDonald Creek as seen from The Loop on Going-to-the-Sun Road. CCC crews who were sent to the fire found almost impossible terrain conditions, but eventually were able to excavate trenches around the smoldering fire. Nonetheless, on August 21, the fire broke out into open burning and men were again dispatched to the fire. They fought the fire, now over 20 acres, on the steep cliffs for nearly a week. On August 25, light rains helped further in controlling the fire. Unfortunately, high winds developed on August 30 and blew the fire across containment lines, endangering many of the 500 CCC boys fighting the fire:

> When their foreman realized their situation, he gave orders to drop most of their tools in the trenches they had built and follow him. He led them into a burned area that was hot but safe. The men stayed together, nobody panicked, and they were all

led to safety. Had they panicked and scattered—as is sometimes the case of pickup fire crews under similar situations some of them would undoubtedly never have come out alive. These boys were, of course, almost scared to death; but they had been trained to follow orders, and it certainly paid off.[8]

Driven by a howling wind, the fire raced down the mountainside and continued up the west side of the Garden Wall below Swiftcurrent Pass, aimed directly for Granite Park Chalet. The employees of the chalet stayed and were prepared to fight the fire to save the building complex, but thanks to the sparse vegetation immediately surrounding the buildings, the fire blew past without damaging any structures there.[9]

Unfortunately, after the fire swept past Granite Park Chalet, it quickly blew over Swiftcurrent Pass around 6 p.m. Within four hours, the fire had blown down the Swiftcurrent valley all the way to the shores of Swiftcurrent Lake, endangering the famous Many Glacier Hotel. On its path there, it burned down the Many Glacier Ranger Station and several outlying structures in that complex, some of the CCC-built Swiftcurrent autocamp cabins, an icehouse by the Many Glacier Hotel, and a saddle-horse corral.[10]

Now August 31, the Many Glacier Hotel was saved through the efforts of employees who remained behind and continuously sprayed the hotel with water from Swiftcurrent Lake and used wet towels and brooms to extinguish burning embers falling on and around the hotel roof. Less fortunate were the Many Glacier Chalets, log structures on the flank of Altyn Peak above the road turn-off to the hotel. All the chalets on the flank of the mountain were burned down by the fire, with only the chalets on the flat surface by Swiftcurrent Falls surviving. Today, you can still find remnants of the chalets such as large nails and spikes, as well as small bits of their interior furnishings such as pieces of china, on the flank of Altyn Peak. Please note that collecting of any such items is forbidden by Park Service regulations.[11]

CCC boys in Camp GNP-4, on the flats below Swiftcurrent Falls, panicked, thinking the fire would continue to press down the valley, and indeed spot fires broke out across the head of Lake Sherburne from the camp. They broke into a room in the camp where guns were kept, told their officers that they were leaving, and fled down valley to Babb. The officers soon followed.[12]

On September 1, the windstorm died down. Moderate rains on the 2nd and heavy rains on the 3rd brought the fire to a close. The devastation from the fire would be visible for decades, although by the 1990s, the valley once again looked green and peaceful. The memory of the fire spurred the building of a fire lookout on a ridge extending northward from Heaven's Park to provide a better high-ground view of the mountainside of Heaven's Peak, the adjacent McDonald Creek valley, and the west side of the Garden Wall where the Going-to-the-Sun Road climbs out of the valley toward Logan Pass. The CCC built a trail most of the way up to the future lookout construction site, but the trail was left unfinished when the CCC was terminated in July 1942.[13]

Left: View of Heaven's Peak and the effects of the 1936 Heaven's Peak fire, taken in 1941 or 1942. (*Ansel Adams photo, U. S. National Archives 519858*)

Below: Granite Park Chalet, shown in this 1939 view, barely survived the Heaven's Peak fire, as the fire passed by within a few tens of meters on its charge up to and over Swiftcurrent Pass and down into the Swiftcurrent valley on the east side. Heaven's Peak is at upper right in the photo (*T. J. Hileman photo, Glacier National Park*)

The Many Glacier Hotel, on the shore of Swiftcurrent Lake in the Swiftcurrent valley in Glacier Park. Fires burned in this valley frequently, as evidenced in this 1933 pre-Heaven's Peak fire photo that shows widespread burned slopes across the lake from the hotel. (*George A. Grant photo, National Park Service*)

This undated photo shows the road leading past the turn-off for the Many Glacier Hotel, on the shore of Swiftcurrent Lake at lower right, to the Swiftcurrent Camp Store and Many Glacier campground at left center. Most of the area left of the road burned in the 1936 Heaven's Peak fire in spite of the firefighting efforts of the CCC and the National Park Service. (*T. J. Hileman photo, Glacier National Park*)

A 1937 view of the Swiftcurrent/Many Glacier Ranger Station area, a year after the 1936 Heaven's Peak fire. It shows a newly reconstructed ranger station and new surrounding buildings. All pre-existing buildings at this site were destroyed by the fire. (*Glacier National Park*)

An undated view of the Many Glacier Chalets, which were located on the flank of Altyn Peak immediately north of the Many Glacier Hotel. All the chalets shown here were destroyed by the Heaven's Peak fire of 1936. (*Great Northern Railway, Minnesota Historical Society I.164.41*)

A 1913 view from the Many Glacier Chalets looking up valley. Swiftcurrent Pass, over which the 1936 Heaven's Peak fire crossed over from the west side of the park, is the low point on the horizon to the left of the lower of the two peak crests shown (Swiftcurrent Mountain). (*Fred Kiser photo, Oregon Historical Society Library ba020940*)

A 1990 view of Swiftcurrent Pass at left center, left of the peak of Swiftcurrent Mountain, and the upper Swiftcurrent valley. Much of the area burned by the Heaven's Peak fire had recovered its forest cover in the intervening years. (*Photo by author, July 17, 1990*)

As a result of the Heaven's Peak fire, a fire lookout was built on a point extending out northward from the main crest of Heaven's Peak. The CCC built the trail to the construction site, but the CCC was disbanded in 1942 before construction on the lookout began. The lookout was completed under the Civilian Public Service program, a program designed for conscientious objectors to work for the country during World War II. (*Glacier National Park photo*)

Fires Along the Middle Fork

Fires in the Middle Fork region of Glacier Park, southeast of Belton/West Glacier and north of Walton Ranger Station, were difficult to fight because of the logistics. CCC boys would drive southeastward on U.S. Highway 2 from Belton, but once arriving as close as possible to the fire site, they had to figure out how to safely cross the railroad tracks of the mainline of the Great Northern Railway. Once that was accomplished, they then had to navigate a crossing of the Middle Fork of the Flathead River to gain access to Glacier Park and the fire sites. River crossings required the construction either of a temporary floating bridge, or transporting a boat by truck to ferry the firefighters and equipment across the Middle Fork. Floating bridges were constructed on site, so it was usually wise to have someone with good carpentry skills in the support crew.

In 1940, a fire was burning on Loneman Mountain in the Nyack region of the Middle Fork. The camp supervisor of CCC Camp GNP-15, a local man named Charles Green, sent a foreman with a twenty-five-man crew to build a floating bridge to get the CCC firefighters across the river. They had a floating bridge of timber and bridge plank built within five hours, allowing trucks to carry equipment and men across the river to near the Loneman Lookout trail where the men then had to hike 5 miles, to within 1 mile of Loneman Lookout, to access the fire.[14]

Not all fire calls on the Middle Fork went as smoothly. At another call to a fire on Loneman Mountain, Charles Green from CCC Camp GNP-15 related how a near disaster was averted during a crossing of the railroad track and subsequent

Fighting fires in the Middle Fork section of Glacier Park was difficult for CCC boys. As shown here in a view looking toward Loneman Mountain and an area burned in 2003, the firefighters had to manage to safely cross the mainline of the Great Northern Railway and subsequently cross the broad floodplain of the Middle Fork of the Flathead River. Loneman Lookout is located on the crest of the mountain. (*Photo by author, July 28, 2009*)

river crossing. Green drove his pickup truck with boat to the crossing site and was accompanied by a young enrollee in an extra truck who would haul the boat back to Camp GNP-15 after Green hiked to the fire site with 100 CCC firefighters. While Green was ferrying men and equipment across the Middle Fork, the truck driver backed his truck down toward the river to receive the boat. Unfortunately, he parked across the tracks of the Great Northern, and a passenger train soon came around the corner and demolished the truck. Fortunately, the young driver leaped clear at the last second. Green gave accident information to the railroad engineer, the young driver returned, shaken but alive, to Belton, and Green went on to cross the river and hike with the 100 CCC boys to the fire site.[15]

Fires Up the North Fork

Fires up the North Fork were somewhat logistically easier than those in the Middle Fork region because the Inside North Fork Road is located east of the North Fork of the Flathead River (and there is no railroad there either) so no river crossings were required. Nonetheless, the North Fork forests are dense and the trail system is limited, so a great deal of hiking and in some cases trailblazing to fire sites was necessary in the area. The glaciated valleys of the North Fork, like the Swiftcurrent valley on the park's east side, are also susceptible to rapid shifts in wind and extremely powerful down valley winds, making firefighting that much more dangerous and unpredictable.

Few accounts of CCC firefighting survive to today, but we again have Charles Green to thank for accounts of North Fork fires and CCC efforts to put them out, again during the dry summer of 1940. One fire was located in the valley above Quartz Lake, an isolated lake south of Bowman Lake. To reach the fire, the CCC crews had to hike from road's end at Bowman Lake over Quartz Ridge to Quartz Lake, and then take a boat from the Quartz Lake Ranger Station 3 miles to the head of the lake. From there, the crews had to blaze a rough trail through the dense forest to the fire in a basin near the base of Vulture Peak. It took most of a week to put out the twenty-acre fire.[16]

Fires above Bowman Lake had their own set of issues. Crews could drive to the foot of Bowman Lake and then take boats to the head of the lake, but then faced several miles of hiking up valley to fire sites, all the while worrying about wind shifts that would bring the fire roaring down the valley. A 1940 summer fire at the foot of the peak called The Guardhouse, on the southside of the valley up beyond the head of Bowman Lake, showed these issues starkly. The fire was burning south of the trail about half a mile in a forest of pitch-rich Engelmann spruce trees that burned "like it was soaked in gasoline." Access to the fire required a 4-mile hike up from the head of the lake, but a shift in the wind caused a thirty-five-man crew to drop their jackets and tools and flee down valley. Fortunately, all made it to safety back to the boats at the head of Bowman Lake.[17]

East Side Fires

The 1936 Heaven's Peak fire's impact on the east side has already been discussed earlier in this chapter. The only other east-side fire with a historical report occurred in the Valentine Creek drainage west of the Waterton River in northern Glacier Park in the summer of 1939. This was a bit of a logistical nightmare to fight. CCC firefighters from Camp GNP-13 on Lake Sherburne in the Swiftcurrent valley were dispatched to fight the fire. Two twenty-five-man crews (most likely "flying squads") were dispatched by the same Charles Green as previously mentioned—Green was camp supervisor at Lake Sherburne in 1939, prior to being appointed camp supervisor at Camp GNP-15 in Belton in 1940.

Green followed the two crews in his pickup truck; they all proceeded to cross the international border at the Chief Mountain border crossing and drove on to Waterton townsite in adjacent Waterton Lakes National Park, Alberta. There, after a steak dinner for all charged to Uncle Sam, they boarded the *International*, the passenger boat that sails on Waterton Lake from Waterton townsite, across the border to the Goat Haunt Ranger Station back in Montana, where they bedded down for the night. The next day, Green and the crew hiked ten miles up the Fifty Mountain/Northern Highline Trail to Valentine Creek, forded the Waterton River, and hiked 4 miles on the Valentine Creek Trail (which leads up to Porcupine Ridge Lookout) to the fire site. After putting out a smoldering ground fire by hauling canvas buckets full of water up a steep cliff to the fire site, they hiked back out and made the trip back to the Swiftcurrent valley in reverse order.[18]

CCC Work on the West Side of Glacier Park

The location of park headquarters—in Belton (West Glacier)—played a strong role in where the CCC camps of the west side were located and where work was carried out. All but one camp, Camp GNP-8 at Anaconda Creek, were within about 7 miles from headquarters (Camp GNP-3 at Fish Creek being the farthest of the "close" camps). Nonetheless, the CCC carried out work on the west side from the Kishehnen Ranger Station in the far northwest corner of the park at what was then the end point of the Inside North Fork Road (the road now ends at the turn-off to Kintla Lake, and only continues as a trail to Kishehnen), to the Walton Ranger Station at the southern tip of the park along U.S. Highway 2.

CCC Work on Fire Clean-up, Revegetation, and Fire Trail Construction

The proximity of most of the west side CCC camps to Belton and Apgar dovetailed nicely with the major work needing to be done as a result of past forest fires. Fire swept through the area in 1910, and in 1926, fire burned a large area between Apgar and the Logging Creek Ranger Station along either side of the Inside North Fork Road. The Half Moon Fire of 1929, only a few years removed from the arrival of the CCC in the summer of 1933, burned over 50,000 acres within Glacier Park after starting outside in the Flathead National Forest. This fire essentially burned the entirety of forest between Belton and Apgar, and the standing dead trees preyed on the mind of the administrators at Belton. The arrival of a large work force that could be used to clear the skeleton trees and re-plant the forest, in the form of CCC boys, was seen as a godsend.[1]

The primary job for the CCC as laid out in 1933 across the western United States was fire prevention and fighting forest fires. However, this quickly morphed into also cleaning up and revegetation after forest fires (a favorite of President Franklin Roosevelt). Trail construction for allowing access to potential future fires in the park's

Above: The 1929 Half Moon Fire, one of the largest in Glacier National Park, is seen here looking from south of Belton northward, toward Lake McDonald. This fire burned virtually the entire area between Belton and Apgar. (*R. E. Marble photo, National Park Service*)

Left: This view of the Half Moon Fire was taken from the Coram Ranger Station about 6 miles southwest of Glacier Park, showing the smoke billowing up in the park. (*K. D. Swan photo, U.S. Forest Service*)

extensive backcountry also was deemed necessary as "fire pre-suppression." Every CCC boy was also trained to fight fires if necessary, as described in the previous chapter.[2]

Hundreds of miles of fire trails were laid out, created, and maintained by CCC boys, especially on the park's west side where tourist hiking trails were fewer in number (numbers of trail-miles constructed by CCC boys in the annual superintendent reports were not always uniformly reported). After the disbanding of the CCC, park trail miles dropped from a high of around 1,000 miles to the current roughly 700 miles, and most of those "lost" trail miles were westside fire trails no longer maintained and allowed to revert to nature. Some can still be found and followed by persons with good wayfinding skills, but others are now completely grown over.

Literally thousands of acres of burned forest from the 1910, 1926, and 1929 Half Moon fires were cleared of burnt, dead trees by workers from Camps GNP-1, GNP-2, GNP-3, and GNP-9. By 1939, "nearly 5,000 acres had been cleared" around the end of Lake McDonald and along the road from Apgar to Belton. Revegetation crews followed the forest clearing crews, planting tree seedlings along the road and around the outlet of the lake. Today, visitors driving from the West Glacier entrance station to the T-intersection with Going-to-the-Sun Road near Apgar pass blissfully ignorant through a forest of lodgepole pines planted in almost perfectly straight rows by CCC boys from the Belton and Apgar camps.[3]

Chopping or sawing down dead, standing trees (called "snags") is hazardous work. During the brief history of the CCC in Glacier Park, three workers were killed by

CCC boys from CCC Camp GNP-1 sawing and chopping down dead trees in the burned-over area of the Half Moon Fire near Belton. (*Glacier National Park*)

CCC worker planting tree seedlings in burned-over area. Seedlings are in the pouch on his belt. It is said that the CCC planted over 2 billion trees nationwide during its short period of existence. (*U.S. National Archives*)

This aerial view of West Glacier shows the location of Park Headquarters above the river, at lower right. Virtually the entire forest from and to the right of the river bridge northward (toward the upper side of the picture) to Lake McDonald (out of sight at upper right) was planted by CCC boys. (*Photo by author, July 26, 1994*)

falling snags while working in the field. On July 20, 1933, William M. Richeson was struck and killed by a falling snag near McDonald Creek in the Half Moon Fire burn scar. William Haynes was killed by a falling snag on September 9, 1934, while working in the Hidden Lake fire scar. Also, on July 7, 1938, Andrew "Jack" Aldrich was hit and killed by a falling snag in the snag removal project in the "Apgar Burn."[4, 5]

Many of the trees cut down by CCC labor were simply burned (especially on the park's east side), but a large amount of timber was salvaged as telephone poles, lumber, and firewood. Westside camps shipped firewood to drought-stricken towns in eastern Montana, as well as to the Blackfeet Reservation east of the park. The Fort Peck Indian Reservation in eastern Montana also received salvaged wood from the park. The Great Northern Railway was used to ship the salvaged firewood. The Blackfeet Reservation also benefitted from more than simply firewood:

> Glacier companies used the railroad to ship poles, fence posts, corral poles, and fire wood to the Blackfeet Reservation. F.R. Stone, the Superintendent of the reservation, claimed that supplying logs and poles to the Indians was "one of the finest things ever done for the Indians on the reservation."[6]

This humanitarian aid to the reservations and communities of eastern Montana is a significant, but unseen today, legacy of the work of the CCC in Glacier Park.

The amount of wood salvaged and processed into lumber, telephone poles, and firewood was impressive. In the 1935 fiscal year, westside camps saved a total of 158 railroad carloads, each weighing 80,000 pounds, of logs, poles, and posts for shipment east. Additional salvaged whole logs were used for construction and for telephone poles in the park. A creosoting facility was established at Camp GNP-1, which in 1933 salvaged 1,978 telephone poles and 117 cords of fire wood.[7]

In 1939, to improve the efficiency of use and reduction of cost of the salvaged dead timber in the Belton to Apgar area, Glacier Park established a sawmill in Camp GNP-1. The park purchased surplus sawmill equipment from Mount Rainier National Park in Washington, and the Fort Peck Dam in eastern Montana. The new sawmill facility greatly improved the speed and reduced the cost and man-hours needed to transform dead timber into lumber:

> From January 1, 1939 to September 30, of that same year, CCC sawyers produced 347,071 board-feet of construction-quality lumber. In fiscal 1941, CCC boys sawed nearly 1,000,000 board-feet of lumber, and 1,686,160 board-feet in fiscal 1942.[8]

CCC Work along the Inside North Fork Road

The Inside North Fork Road basically parallels the North Fork of the Flathead River from Fish Creek, on the north side of Lake McDonald, all the way to the turn-off to Kintla Lake. During CCC days, the road extended to the Kishehnen Ranger Station just south of the Canadian border.

Most of the work along the Inside North Fork Road was carried out by CCC workers from Camp GNP-3 at Fish Creek or Camp GNP-8 at Anaconda Creek. The area along the road between these two camps had burned in the large 1926 forest fire, leaving a landscape of dead trees that continuously threatened to fall across and block the road. Workers from the two camps labored at clearing the dead trees along the road as well as re-stringing telephone lines along the road that seemed to be in constant need of repair. As an example of the extensive work carried out in this area, in the first year of the CCC in the park in 1933, the Fish Creek camp workers cleared 93 acres of forest burned in the 1926 fire and replaced two-and-a-half miles of telephone line along the Inside Road. Farther north, the CCC workers from the Anaconda Creek camp built 6 miles of fire trail connecting North Fork valleys and to the road near Anaconda Creek, cleared 10 miles of forest along the Inside Road, and also re-aligned 7 miles of the road.[9]

If you have camped or used pit toilets virtually anywhere at or north of Fish Creek along the Inside North Fork Road, you have benefitted from CCC work. CCC workers improved campsites, installed picnic tables and cooking grates, and dug garbage pits and pit toilets (outhouses) at Bowman Lake, Bowman Creek, Kintla Lake, Quartz Creek, and Fish Creek campgrounds. Ranger stations also benefitted along the entire Inside Road, with landscape clearing and maintenance, horse corral maintenance and repair, and construction of fireguard caches and woodsheds.[10]

CCC boys from several camps, including especially the camps at Fish Creek (GNP-3) and Anaconda Creek (GNP-8), cleared several miles of burned and down deadwood from the 1926 and 1929 fires along the Inside North Fork Road. This view shows the state of the road and surrounding forest after the 1926 fire. (*Glacier National Park HPF2153*)

Above: This downstream view from the Camas Creek bridge on the Inside North Fork Road shows little evidence of the 1926 and 1929 fires. (*Photo by author, July 26, 1994*)

Below left: The Inside North Fork Road at the CCC GNP-8, Anaconda Creek, site shows the effects of the clearing of the burned deadwood. (*Photo by author, July 26, 1994*)

Below right: At the Logging Creek Ranger Station on the Inside North Fork Road, CCC boys built several of the buildings around the Ranger Station, shown at left center. (*Photo by author, July 26, 1994*)

This fireguard cabin at Logging Creek Ranger Station was built by the CCC. (*National Park Service*)

Kishehnen Ranger Station complex at north end of Inside North Fork Road as it existed in the 1930s (the road now ends at the turn-off for the Kintla Lake road). Fireguard/fire cache and woodshed structures were built by CCC crews here and at every other ranger station along the Inside North Fork Road. (*George A. Grant photo, National Park Service*)

CCC Work in the Belton Headquarters Area

The main entrance to the west side of Glacier National Park is across the Middle Fork of the Flathead River north of the village of Belton (West Glacier). On April 7, 1941, work began on an entrance station structure where the increasing amount of automobile traffic would receive information and pay entrance fees. Rocks for the entrance station were mined locally outside the park, where because of the nature of the rocks along U.S. Highway 2 southeast of Belton, a free source of material was available:

> Elmer Fladmark, the Chief Ranger at the time, went over the plans with me during that winter, and I told him where we could get the rock for free. Funds were available to hire a rock mason and two carpenters, and I asked for 2 men who were masters at their trade. Ole Nordeen was to do the rock work, and as soon as the snow went off that spring, we got Ole and went up to inspect the rock.
>   The location was a rock cut above Nyack on U.S. Highway 2 where the solid rock from highway construction was broken in rectangular pieces. The Park Superintendent told me he wished I had told him of this simple precaution 2 years before.... Ole showed me the type of pieces he wanted, and I found a slope where trucks could be driven below the highway for access.... Two large dump trucks were assigned to haul the rock, and one of these hauled a small dozer to smooth the road.... In three months the building was completed and in use.[11, 12]

A secondary entrance kiosk was added after World War II, to accommodate the post-war increase in traffic to the park. That kiosk also allowed for the entrance of large recreational vehicles that became increasingly popular in the 1950s and 1960s.

The new park entrance station at the Belton entrance was by no means the only work carried out by the CCC in what is now West Glacier. Indeed, the headquarters area comprises the Glacier National Park Headquarters Historic District, listed in the National Register of Historic Places since 1996. The structures in the historic district are a combination of architecture and landscape styles from three general eras—the pre-CCC 1920s; the CCC era, during which perhaps half of the buildings in the district were built; and the Mission 66-era 1960s. The National Park Service provides a written and audio walking tour for visitors interested in viewing the visual mélange of buildings comprising the headquarters area.

The Community Building in the headquarters district serves as the "heart and soul" for the small park service community. The building has an interesting history because it was not built by the CCC and was originally located in Apgar:

> In 1938 the headquarters area acquired the community building. This building originally stood in Apgar. Built in 1923 by the Gold Brothers as part of the Transmountain Hotel complex it had been known as "Gold's Bungalow" and had functioned as dance hall and entertainment center for Apgar for several years. In the aftermath of the Half Moon Fire, the Gold family sold its property to the federal

Aerial view of West Glacier shows the Park Headquarters complex at far right-center. The village of West Glacier is to the left of the river, Belton Station is adjacent and to the left of the railroad tracks at lower left. U.S. Highway 2 runs diagonally across the lower left of the photo. The park entrance station is in the thick forest near the right edge of the picture. (*Photo by author, July 26, 1994*)

Above left: The rocks for the West Glacier entrance station were mined locally by a CCC crew in the Nyack area along U.S. Highway 2. The rocks there provided rectangular slabs suitable for construction. The specific site is unspecified, but this cut near Coal Creek meets the criteria described by CCC Foreman Charles Green in his memoir. (*Photo by author, July 21, 1999*)

Above right: West Glacier entrance station, showing the kiosk addition on the right that allowed creation of an additional traffic entrance lane. (*Glacier National Park*)

West Glacier entrance station to Glacier National Park, built by the CCC, was begun on April 7, 1941, and completed that summer. (*Glacier National Park Annual Report, 1941*)

West Glacier entrance station, *c.* 1960, looking northward toward Apgar. Even with the addition of the kiosk, traffic backs up during peak times. (*Jack E. Boucher photo, National Park Service public domain*)

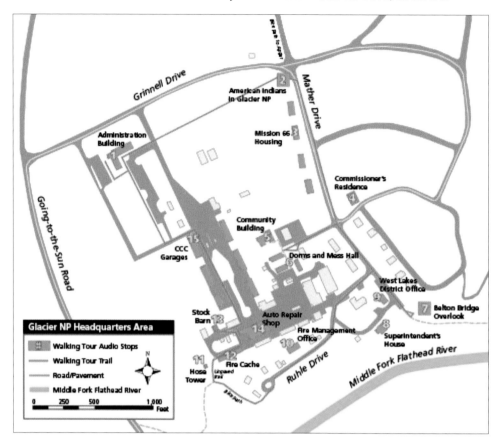

Map of the West Glacier Headquarters historic district, including CCC-built garages and the Community Center relocated by the CCC from Apgar to headquarters. (*Glacier National Park*)

government for $35,000. While most of the cabin camp buildings were subsequently sold for almost nothing and razed for salvage, the bungalow was left standing. By the mid 1930s, park administrators perceived the need for a "community building" in the headquarters residential area and eyed the bungalow as one option for fulfilling that need. Although government policy did not allow allocation of funds for construction of new community building, park administrators found a way around that regulation by defining the building as a "conference training center". A CCC crew cut the building into sections and moved it from Apgar to the headquarters area in 1938. The building was then reassembled and remodeled. While it did see much use for training of personnel, it was used more regularly for a variety of community functions, including weekly movie screening during the summer months and children roller-skating in the dark and damp winter months.[13]

The building continues to serve as a training, conference, and community facility. In September 2005, it hosted an academic workshop on alpine tree line and tree line changes caused by climate change that I co-organized and co-hosted with colleagues from the universities of Iowa and North Carolina and the U.S. Geological Survey.

Community Center, Park Headquarters. Built in Apgar as part of the Gold Brothers hotel complex in 1923, it was moved to the headquarters area in 1938 by the CCC. (*Charles Swaney photo, Creative Commons*)

Numerous buildings throughout the headquarters historic district were, however, built by the CCC. Some are quite unique, such as the hose tower built in 1934 for drying fire hoses, whereas others such as the warehouse and equipment garages (built in 1941) are quite mundane and much the same as those constructed at St. Mary. Several new residence cottages were added to the residential area by the CCC in 1936 as well. The CCC also retrofitted nearly all residences (that did not have one) with a garage—a sign of the new era of family automobile dependence. A number of old woodsheds were also torn down, replaced instead by new combination woodshed-and-garage structures.[14]

In addition to building structures, CCC boys from Camp GNP-1 carried out a significant amount of landscaping and beautification in the headquarters district. They put in rock-lined flagstone sidewalks in the summer of 1934, lined footpaths and driveways with cobbles, planted seedlings around homes, and protected those seedlings from animals with protective wire nets. Large, attractive streetlamps were also installed in the residential area. In total, over 20 acres of headquarters-area cleanup and landscaping was completed by the CCC.[15, 16]

Not all the CCC work in the headquarters area resulted in buildings and landscaping. CCC boys constructed a large water supply system for headquarters that involved over a mile of trenching, pipe installation, and burial to tap into McDonald Creek for water. CCC labor was also used at park headquarters, to relieve the over-worked rangers and other staff from some mundane tasks. CCC boys were taught and learned skills such as typewriting and office work. They were also taught how to use the park radio system and radio broadcasting, relieving rangers from the necessity of staffing the park radio station. CCC boys trained in radio skills at headquarters were subsequently distributed to ranger stations around the park, again to alleviate the workload on the rangers at those outposts.[17]

Left: Tower for hanging and drying fire hoses, built in 1933 by the CCC and still used today. (*Charles Swaney photo, Creative Commons*)

Below: Another view of the unusual CCC-built fire hose tower with connecting footbridge into the structure. (*Claire Harbage, National Public Radio*)

CCC warehouse building in the Park Headquarters garage area. (*Charles Swaney photo, Creative Commons*)

Garages in the Park Headquarters historic district, built by the CCC in the early 1940s. (*Charles Swaney photo, Creative Commons*)

CCC-built garages dating to the early 1940s, with part of the Belton Hills in the distance. (*Charles Swaney photo, Creative Commons*)

One of four combination woodshed/garage structures built in the Park Headquarters area by the CCC. (*Glacier National Park Annual Report, 1937*)

CCC crews are believed to have been the primary workers involved with construction of headquarters sidewalks and installation of street lamps. View north along Mather Drive. (*Glacier National Park HPF 1904, Glacier National Park Annual Report, 1938*)

CCC boys were trained to work the communications and broadcast equipment in Park Headquarters, in order to free up park personnel from this duty. (*Glacier National Park Annual Report, 1938*)

Additional Work on the West Side

A variety of non-construction-related tasks were also carried out by CCC boys across the western side of Glacier Park. Blister rust control, described in more detail in chapter six, took place in the McDonald Creek valley and around park headquarters. As one example, in 1941, CCC workers carried out the clearing of 1,159 acres of blister rust in the McDonald Creek valley. Other years also saw westside blister rust control work, but superintendent reports from those years did not specify locations nor acreage.[18]

CCC workers were heavily involved in major campground construction and improvement for camping sites along Going-to-the-Sun Road. Sprague Creek and Avalanche Creek Campgrounds were enlarged by CCC boys in 1935. Work in those campgrounds included installation of camp cooking grates, picnic tables, and water systems with "comfort stations" and fire hydrants. A new campground at the foot of Lake McDonald, now known as the Apgar Campground, was carried out in 1939. Water lines were laid in the Apgar and Avalanche Campgrounds in 1940, including 5,000 feet of water line at Avalanche and 10,000 feet at Apgar Campground.[19, 20, 21]

Every year, considerable road clearance and clean-up on Going-to-the-Sun Road was carried out by CCC boys. Some years, specific stretches of road cleanup were described in the annual superintendent reports, but in others, only general comments on roadside cleanup were given. Mileages of cleanup were sometimes mentioned but without specific locations (in general, the annual reports from Superintendent Libbey from 1939 onward were much less specific and less detailed than the reports from 1933 to 1938 from Superintendent Scoyen). In 1940, for example, a total of 16 miles of roadside cleanup was accomplished between park headquarters and Avalanche Creek.[22]

One structure completed by the CCC in the Lake McDonald Lodge Historic District is notable for its beauty and illustration of the skill of CCC labor—the bridge over Snyder Creek on the secondary road in front of Lake McDonald Lodge. The bridge is still standing proudly today, although most tourists who drive through the Lake McDonald Lodge complex are unaware of its history and significance:

> Civilian Conservation Corp crews ... constructed the lower Snyder Creek Bridge in 1935 along the Lake McDonald Lodge secondary access road (originally the Going-to-the-Sun Road). The bridge replaced a smaller wooden structure constructed in the 1920s. Replacement of existing log retaining walls with stone rip rap was included in the bridge construction plans.
>
> The Snyder Creek Bridge is a significant example of rustic stone architecture. It is located in a cedar grove, just upstream from the cedar-and-stone Snyder dormitory and the cedar-and-stone auditorium. The stones used in the foundations and in the bridge and associated rip rap are clearly evident along the creek bed and banks. This concentrated use of native materials within a stone-and-cedar-filled setting is a remarkable example of the successful application of rustic-architecture's central tenant to "harmonize improvements with the landscape."[23]

Snyder Creek bridge in the Lake McDonald historic district, built by the CCC in 1935–1936. (*National Park Service*)

Trail maintenance, new trails construction (mostly, but not completely, fire trails), and snow removal in advance of each summer tourist season were carried out across the west side of the park by the CCC boys. One example of non-fire trail construction was the trail to Scalplock Lookout, near the Walton Ranger Station at the southern tip of the park. CCC boys created the trail to Scalplock Lookout that still exists today. The trail climbs 2,900 vertical feet, over a series of seventeen switchbacks, to the crest of the peak and the lookout at 6,919 feet.[24]

Snow removal by CCC boys was concentrated along stretches of the Highline Trail, including the area north of Granite Park Chalet around the infamous, very steep, Ahern Drift. That drift, as well as other steep drifts along the trail, often require dynamite blasting in order to loosen the compacted and hardened snow sufficiently for subsequent shoveling and removal. CCC boys were trained in the use of dynamite for trail clearing, but such a dangerous substance inevitably led to one unfortunate situation. CCC enrollee Robert E. McBroom was severely injured while blasting dynamite near Ahern Pass. "He suffered a brain concussion, multiple fractures of the left hand, and total loss of eyesight". He was subsequently allotted $22 a month as compensation.[25]

One other CCC task carried out that is not obvious today, nor likely to visitors of the time, was providing manpower for search-and-rescue operations. Glacier Park in the 1930s was very short on staff for such necessary activities, and again the presence of the CCC was seen as a godsend by park administrators. Missing hikers and other tourists could be sought by CCC crews whenever needed over summer visitor seasons.

Above left: CCC workers creating the trail to Scalplock Lookout in the southernmost part of Glacier Park. The trail, still used today, climbs 2,900 vertical feet over a series of seventeen switchbacks, to the crest of the peak and the lookout at 6,919 feet. (*U.S. Forest Service*)

Above right: CCC crew on a search-and-rescue mission on the west side of the Garden Wall below the Highline Trail in Glacier Park, August 1, 1936. (*Photo by Chris Fitzgerald and "Building America—The CCC"*)

One example of this occurred in 1936, unfortunately with no happy outcome. Herbert Gray, a teenager from Maine, left the Granite Park Chalet on July 26, 1936, heading southward to climb the Garden Wall above the Highline Trail. Portions of the Garden Wall are quite steep and abundant loose rock and slippery meltwater streams characterize the steep slopes. Gray never returned to the chalet. On August 1, a CCC search team was dispatched, searching up to 8,500 feet in elevation, but no trace of the young man was found by the CCC search crew. Gray's body was finally found on August 12, 1 mile southeast of Granite Park Chalet, where he had apparently fallen from a cliff and died.[26, 27]

CCC Work in the Logan Pass Area

Logan Pass is the high point on Going-to-the-Sun Road, situated at 6,646 feet above sea level on the Continental Divide separating the west side of the park from the east side. As such, it is neither truly east nor west, so we will examine the work done by the CCC at and around Logan Pass separately from either side of the park. The work at Logan Pass is not immediately apparent, no structures were built by the CCC there, nor is there any obvious clearing and replanting of vegetation. Nonetheless, the CCC has a rich history at this location worthy of a closer look.

Soon after the arrival of CCC boys in Glacier Park in the early summer of 1933, a ceremony for the completion of Going-to-the-Sun Road was planned for Logan Pass on July 15, 1933. Thousands of people—including dignitaries; representatives of local Native American tribes, including a Blackfeet Tribal Band; and a chorus comprised of CCC boys—were to attend. Such a large crowd required extensive snow removal for parking, the ceremonial site, room for tipis for the Native American delegations, and tents for the spike camp of CCC workers who were to prepare the site. CCC boys provided the necessary labor to prepare the site for the July 15 ceremonies.

The dedication ceremony began with a picnic lunch. A chili lunch was prepared for 2,500 people, but they ran out of food when over 4,000 actually showed up. Lunch was followed by a formal program overseen by Glacier Park Superintendent E. T. Scoyen. Dignitaries gave speeches, the Blackfeet Tribal Band played several selections, and the CCC chorus sang a song just before the road was formally dedicated. Although weather conditions at Logan Pass can be "iffy" even in the middle of summer, excellent weather with "decorator clouds" characterized the afternoon proceedings.[1]

The primary association of the CCC with Logan Pass is not, however, the dedication ceremony but an amazing job that today is virtually undetectable by park visitors. The work of the CCC boys made possible the first cross-park, trans-mountain telephone line connecting West Glacier with St. Mary. This line was critical for allowing the new district office in St. Mary to communicate easily with park headquarters in Belton (West Glacier), and was an indispensable component for communications and subsequent dispersal of CCC firefighters during fire season.

Above left: Snow clearance on July 12, 1933, in advance of the dedication ceremony for Going-to-the-Sun Road at Logan Pass to be held on July 15. Although not stated in the original photo caption, the workers clearing the snow were almost assuredly CCC boys. (*George A. Grant photo, GLAC 11419*)

Above right: Aerial view of the Sun Road dedication ceremony, July 15, 1933. (*Glacier National Park GLAC 15557b*)

Another aerial view of the Sun Road dedication ceremony, with tipis from the Blackfeet and Flathead tribes in attendance and performing at lower left. Tents in the lower center probably housed CCC boys working and performing at the ceremony. (*Glacier National Park GLAC 15557c*)

At Logan Pass, elevation 6,654 feet, on the Continental Divide

Saturday, July Fifteenth
Nineteen Thirty-three

E. T. SCOYEN, *Superintendent*
Glacier National Park

Firefighters' Lunch .... 12 o'Clock Noon
Raising of the Flag.............2 o'Clock P. M.

PROGRAM

Introductory Remarks......................E. T. Scoyen
Presentation of Distinguished Guests ....E. T. Scoyen
Selection..........................Blackfeet Tribal Band

Unveiling of Stephen T. Mather Plaque

"Stephen T. Mather"...................O. S. Warden,
Chairman, Montana Highway Commission

Ten Minutes with the Waterton-Glacier
International Peace Park

Selection..........................Blackfeet Tribal Band
"The International Park....Brig.-Gen. J. S. Stewart and
W. A. Buchanan, *Alberta Senators*

Dedication of the
Going-to-the-Sun Highway

Song.............. Chorus, Civilian Conservation Corps
"Construction of the Highway".. W. H. Lynch, District
Engineer, United States Bureau of Public Roads

Above left: Going-to-the-Sun Road, the famous trans-park road of Glacier National Park, was dedicated on July 15, 1933, at Logan Pass. This is the front cover from the dedication ceremony program. (*Glacier National Park Annual Report, 1933*)

Above right: A CCC choir sang at the Sun Road dedication ceremony, as listed in the order of program. (*Glacier National Park Annual Report, 1933*)

The dedication ceremony of Going-to-the-Sun Road at Logan Pass, looking eastward toward the St. Mary valley, July 15, 1933. (*Photo by George A. Grant, National Park Service photo Grant 626*)

Visitors eating lunch in the meadows at Logan Pass during the Sun Road dedication ceremony, July 15, 1933. (*Photo by George A. Grant, Glacier National Park GLAC 11428*)

In order to connect the west side of the park with the east side via telephone, phone lines had to be strung or laid across the Continental Divide. Deciding that phone poles with hanging lines would be far too unsightly along Going-to-the-Sun Road, most of the line needed to be buried. In his 1939 Superintendent's Report, which (because fiscal years in that period ran from June 1 to May 31) covered the CCC work in the summer of 1938, new Superintendent D. S. Libbey noted:

> Construction of more than three hundred miles of new telephone lines was accomplished during the 1939 fiscal year. This included a telephone line across the Continental Divide from Park Headquarters to Lake McDonald Hotel to St. Mary. Approximately 3,500 feet of underground cable were laid from Hidden Lake to Logan Pass.[2]

Superintendent Libbey's three-sentence report on the construction masked an enormous effort by the CCC boys. The sheer scale of this effort is revealed in greater detail in two additional reports by authors examining the history of the CCC. One of these reports states:

> Enrollees at Hidden Lake laid twenty-eight tons of underground phone cable for seven miles over Logan Pass while other companies scaled 500 foot steel ladders …

to measure the amount of cable required on the sheer cliffs of the Continental Divide. This "impossible feat" drew congratulatory comments from Park Service engineers who toured the site at the end of the season.[3]

The second report provides even more detailed information about the work between Logan Pass and Hidden Pass:

> CCC crews from GNP-11, Roes Creek, built a ... circuit of lead-coated heavy copper cable over Logan Pass via Avalanche Creek and Hidden Lake. To move the cable into position, sixty-four enrollees each carried forty-five pounds of cable over the 7,000+ foot pass at a time. In all, enrollees moved eighteen tons of cable by hand for this project. One and one-half miles of cable stretched from Avalanche Creek Campground to the 1,000' cliff near Hidden Lake. The CCCs buried all of the cable from this project to protect it from wind and avalanche danger and to preserve the back country's pristine nature.[4]

The discrepancy in the amount of tonnage of underground phone cable (28 tons *v.* 18 tons) listed in the two reports may, perhaps, be attributable to the first report including all the cable from Avalanche campground up to the cliffs below Hidden Lake versus the second report only listing the amount of cable carried and buried from Logan Pass to Hidden Pass by CCC workers from Camp GNP-11 (Roes Creek). It is also unclear which CCC camp supplied the labor for the work from Avalanche campground to the cliffs below Hidden Lake. It seems unlikely that boys from Camp GNP-11 from Roes Creek did this work given the large additional miles of driving it would have taken to deliver the workers across the Continental Divide and down to Avalanche; more likely, it was a group of workers coming up from one or more of the camps at Belton or Apgar.

Imagine the logistics involved in carrying tons of telephone cable up the Hidden Lake trail from Logan Pass to Hidden Pass. If you have ever hiked this trail, it is about 1.5 miles from Logan Pass to the Hidden Lake Overlook just across Hidden Pass. Did you labor and breathe heavily, perhaps with some stops to gasp a bit for air? Now, imagine doing that hike as one of sixty-four equally spaced hikers, each of whom was carrying 45 pounds of cable, doing so in synchronization. Also, if you have hiked this trail (I have done so at least half a dozen times), did you ever see any signs of the buried phone cable? I never did, although recent Park Service photographs illustrate erosion that has revealed the cable near Hidden Pass. Did you see any signs of the outdoor lunch area, set up with benches holding tubs of cold drinks and food? Again, neither did I—a testament to the amazing efforts by both the CCC and National Park Service in removing any trace of this monumental CCC project.

CCC workers carry the trans-mountain telephone cable towards Hidden Pass from Logan Pass, 1938. Clements Mountain is the prominent peak at center rear. (*Glacier National Park HPF 4568*)

Clements Mountain and the general route of the trans-mountain telephone cable in 2009. (*Photo by author, July 30, 2009*)

CCC workers carry telephone cable along the glacial moraine at the base of Clements Mountain as they approach Hidden Lake Pass, 1938. (*Glacier National Park*)

CCC workers carry the trans-mountain telephone cable along the flank of the Clements Mountain moraine, 1938. View is looking downslope toward Logan Pass. (*Glacier National Park Annual Report, 1939*)

Lunchtime for the CCC telephone cable work crew at Logan Pass, 1938. (*George A. Grant photo, National Park Service*)

View of the general area at Logan Pass where CCC lunchtimes were held. (*Photo by author, July 29, 2000*)

7

CCC Work on the East Side of Glacier Park

The work carried out by the CCC in Glacier Park east of the Continental Divide differed somewhat from that on the west side of the park. Similarities included fighting fires and cleaning up burned forests after forest fires, but the smaller, less dense forests of the east side of the park translated into differences in the need for construction of fire trails. Far fewer fire trails were built on the east side in comparison to the dense network that had been created along and east of the Inside North Fork Road on the west side. This pattern was aided by the presence of a greater network of tourist trails on the east side, allowing CCC boys better access to forested sites without the need for widespread fire trail construction. East-side work that was also similar to that of the westside included campground clearance and construction, planting of trees in the newly created campgrounds, laying of water and sewer lines at several locations including St. Mary, Roes Creek, Many Glacier, and Glacier Park Station (East Glacier), construction of weather station instrument shelters and guard fences for six weather-data-gathering sites (west side at headquarters in Belton, Apgar, and Polebridge, and east side at Belly River, St. Mary, and Glacier Park Station), and stringing telephone lines.

One of the largest phone line projects on the east side was stringing the telephone line 45 miles from Glacier Park Station northward to Kennedy Creek. CCC boys from several of the east-side camps also worked to mark out and clear a swath designating the boundary between the Blackfeet Indian Reservation and the park.

Nonetheless, because of the drier nature of the forest on the east of the park, along with a higher level of afternoon thunderstorm activity, east-side fires could start quickly and spread rapidly if unobserved. A network of fire lookout structures had been built on the west side of the park in the late 1920s and early 1930s before the creation of the CCC, but prior to 1933, there were no fire lookouts on the east side of the park. One of the early jobs of the CCC on the east side was, therefore, constructing fire lookouts.[1]

East Side Fire Lookouts

The Curly Bear Lookout was one of the first lookout structures built by the CCC on the east side. Workers from Camps GNP-4 and GNP-5 in the Swiftcurrent valley near Many Glacier were involved in the lookout construction as well as the stringing of telephone wire from the Red Eagle Lake trail to the lookout (see the map at the front of this book for the lookout location southeast of St. Mary Lake; all lookouts on the map are shown with black triangles within circle symbols). The editor of the camp newspaper for CCC Camps GNP-4 and GNP-5, *Glacier Ice Sheet*, wrote a story about the drive from the Swiftcurrent valley down past Lower St. Mary Lake to the Red Eagle Lake lane/trail east of St. Mary Lake, in which he described the outstanding mountain scenery along the way. His tone changed when it came time to lay out over 4 miles of telephone line from the Red Eagle trail to the base of Curly Bear Mountain:

> After getting our bearings we were ready to start chaining the length of this trail. Traversing this forest with its jungle of scrub brush, fallen timber, thorn bush, and ravines filled with running water is not pleasant to speak about. These things and the mosquitoes constantly buzzing around and making life miserable for a person is the penalty we pay to nature for the privilege of viewing its majestic glory.[2]

The Curly Bear Lookout commanded an outstanding view of the slopes below Curly Bear Mountain and across St. Mary Lake. The lookout was built in the summer of 1934 and was used through the summer of 1959. Having fallen into disrepair by then, it was burned down by the National Park Service in 1963. Today, the view across St. Mary Lake from along Going-to-the-Sun Road shows no trace of the lookout site nor the trail that led to it.[3]

This view of Singleshot Mountain on the left provides a profile of what a CCC worker called "the Nun's Head" on his way to lay 4 miles of phone cable to Curly Bear Lookout above St. Mary Lake. Legend also says this is a profile of the Blackfeet deity Napi. (*Photo by author, July 30, 2007*)

A view downslope to Curly Bear Lookout with St. Mary Lake in the distance. The lookout was built by CCC workers in 1934. (*Glacier National Park photo HPF 9520*)

The Curly Bear Lookout, built by the CCC, was located at the base of Curly Bear Mountain, shown here south of St. Mary Lake. The lookout was destroyed by the Park Service in 1963. (*Photo by author, July 23, 1990*)

Another lookout built by the CCC was the Bear Mountain Lookout near the Canadian border in the northeastern part of Glacier Park. This lookout was built in the summer of 1935, probably by CCC boys in a spike camp out of the Swiftcurrent valley Camps GNP-4 and GNP-5 (they were the closest main camps to this site, although no information exists as to where the workers here actually came from). This lookout was built to provide views to the northeast along the newly constructed Chief Mountain International Highway, as well as into the adjacent Mokowanis River valley and the area around the Crossley (Cosley) Lake Tent Camp. Bear Mountain Lookout was only staffed from 1935 to 1953, and it too was burned down by the National Park Service, in 1966.[4]

The Porcupine Ridge Lookout was the last lookout built by the CCC, although CCC boys also worked on the trail leading up to the site of the future Heaven's Peak Lookout subsequently built by conscientious objectors in the Civilian Public Service during World War II. Built in the summer of 1939 by CCC boys in a spike camp at Goathaunt on the southern end of Waterton Lake, the Porcupine Ridge Lookout is located on a ridge north of Valentine Creek and provides broad views of that creek valley, the Waterton River valley, and across to the slopes surrounding the park's highest peak, Mt. Cleveland. First staffed in 1940, it has recently been renovated to serve as a communications center for border security purposes and observation in the post-9/11 world.[5]

The CCC-ID was also involved in the construction of fire lookouts. A metal fire tower was constructed from a kit and emplaced on a high point of Swiftcurrent Ridge almost directly west of the small Blackfeet Reservation village of Babb. This lookout offered an unobstructed view of the entire eastern front of Glacier Park's forest from Napi Point and East Flattop Mountain on the south to Sherburne Peak on the north, as well as reservation forests east of the park boundary. The tower was apparently emplaced in 1937 under the supervision of Superintendent C. L. Graves of the "Blackfoot Ind. Agency" of "Fort Browning" (Browning). However, its origin was somewhat lost over the years until rediscovered in 1959. That year, through an interagency agreement between the Blackfeet people and the National Park Service, the tower was removed from Swiftcurrent Ridge and moved to Red Eagle Meadow on the southern shore of St. Mary Lake in Glacier Park. During the move, markings were discovered on the tower indicating its origin and placement by the CCC-ID. After the move to Red Eagle Meadow, the tower served only until its subsequent removal from the park in October 1986.[6,7]

A Blackfeet Indian Service wooden lookout on the Glacier Park/Blackfeet Reservation boundary on Divide Mountain was built in 1934, but it is not clear if it was built by CCC-ID workers. CCC-ID workers did maintain the phone line from the lookout to the CCC-ID camp at the base of Divide Mountain. The camp was therefore in direct communication with the lookout on the mountain ridge above and with the National Park Service.[8,9]

Looking up at the CCC-built Bear Mountain Lookout from below. (*Glacier National Park HPF 1145*)

Bear Mountain Lookout above the Belly River valley in northeastern Glacier National Park, built by the CCC in 1935. (*Photo by R. A. Nelson, Glacier National Park HPF 5791*)

Above: Porcupine Ridge Lookout under construction. The lookout was built by CCC labor, completed in 1938, and used for the first time in 1939. (*Glacier National Park*)

Left: The completed Porcupine Ridge Lookout is shown here in 1940. The lookout is a variation on the style of lookouts built at Apgar, Mount Brown, and Loneman. The catwalk was not as effectively supported, and the roof is at a gentler angle but does not extend out over the catwalk as at the Scalplock, Huckleberry, and Numa Ridge Lookouts. (*Glacier National Park*)

Looking across Lower St. Mary Lake to the former location of the Swiftcurrent Ridge Lookout, located on the crest of the green ridge at upper center. The lookout was installed as a CCC-ID project overseen by C. L. Graves, superintendent of what at the time was called the "Blackfoot Indian Agency." (*Photo by author, September 4, 2004*)

View from the Swiftcurrent Ridge Lookout to the west, with Lake Sherburne at right center, 1954. Although located on the Blackfeet Reservation, the lookout was used primarily to monitor forest conditions in Glacier National Park. (*Photo by H. E. Malde, U.S. Geological Survey*)

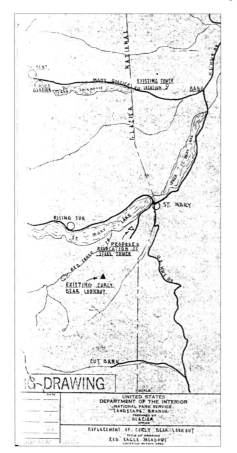 

Above left: In 1959, the National Park Service proposed moving the Swiftcurrent Ridge Lookout to Red Eagle Meadow to replace the Curly Bear Lookout. The circle near the top of the map that shows the "existing tower location" is almost directly west of the town of Babb, and an empty triangle near the center of the map marks the "proposed relocation of steel tower" south of St. Mary Lake. (*Glacier National Park GLAC 18240*)

Above right: The Swiftcurrent Ridge Lookout was moved in 1959 to Red Eagle Meadow, shown here near St. Mary, in Glacier National Park. The CCC identification information from its installation on Swiftcurrent Ridge was discovered when the tower was moved. (*Rocky Mountain Regional Office, National Park Service*)

CCC Work in the Swiftcurrent Valley

The Swiftcurrent valley is the most popular destination in Glacier National Park after the Going-to-the-Sun Road from Belton/West Glacier to St. Mary. At the heart of the valley is the Many Glacier Hotel and the nearby Swiftcurrent Motor Inn and Campstore. From these locations, a large network of trails radiates into surrounding valleys, leading to popular hiking locations including Cracker Lake, Piegan Pass, Grinnell Glacier and Lake, Swiftcurrent Pass, Iceberg Lake, and Ptarmigan Lake and Tunnel. Virtually every one of these trails were worked on and improved by CCC labor.

Lake Sherburne and the Lake Sherburne dam site are encountered about halfway up the Many Glacier road, just before the park boundary and nearby entrance station. The dam was built between 1914 and 1921, creating a lake when full that stretches up valley toward Many Glacier—a distance of almost 6 miles. The dam is located outside the park on the Blackfeet Reservation and thus did not require approval from Glacier National Park; it was also built during the early years of the park and was initiated before the creation of the National Park Service in 1916. The lake impounds water that is part of the U.S. Bureau of Reclamation's Milk River Project, which provides waters to farmers in north-central Montana. Due to irrigation drawdown, lake levels can be quite low in late summer and autumn.

The creation of Lake Sherburne drowned a large number of trees along the shores of the new reservoir. Many of these dead trees also fell into the lake, creating a large amount of floating woody debris. Between skeleton trees on the lakeshore and woody debris that could float down the lake and threaten to clog the dam intake/water release openings, many CCC boys from Camps GNP-4 and GNP-5 located on the north shore of Lake Sherburne spent a great deal of time clearing floating debris and chopping down and removing dead standing trees. This was ongoing work requiring attention virtually every summer during the period of the CCC's existence. Crews from Camp GNP-4 also were involved outside the park boundary in repairing siphon tubes that transferred water from the St. Mary River, downstream near the village of Babb, to the Milk River drainage for irrigation purposes.[10, 11]

As mentioned earlier, life in the CCC was not without its dangers, and Lake Sherburne could be a dangerous place. Winds often howl down the valley from the mountains at near-hurricane strength, driving woody debris down the lake to the dam intake and causing extremely "choppy" conditions on the lake. Wind conditions were not reported on the day of multiple fatalities there, but on July 24, 1934, a launch carrying lunch and lemonade in tall milk cans to a crew clearing the park boundary on the far side of the dam capsized into Lake Sherburne. The launch operator apparently engaged in "horseplay," which caused the tall milk cans to shift and the launch to tip over, dumping all seven men on the boat into the cold water. Three drowned, including the launch operator, while the other four were able to swim to shore.[12, 13]

Progressing up valley, the CCC was responsible for a great deal of trail maintenance on the trails emanating out of the Many Glacier/Swiftcurrent area. This work involved clearing of downed trees across trails, smoothing and widening trails, brush removal, and erosion control. A great deal of removal of burned trees from the 1936 Heaven's Peak Fire and earlier fires was carried out around the area of the present-day Many Glacier Campground and up onto the lower slopes of Grinnell Point. In 1933, as just one example of the tree-clearing work typically carried out every summer by one individual camp, CCC boys from Camp GNP-4 cleared over 54 acres of burned logs and stumps around the base of Grinnell Mountain.[14]

Building construction and campground clearance in the area of present-day Swiftcurrent were important jobs carried out by the CCC. The CCC built the original Swiftcurrent Motor Inn building. They also built loops of "housekeeping cabins" at Swiftcurrent as well as the shower and laundry building there. Nearby, the new

Lake Sherburne, looking westward toward Many Glacier, 1941. CCC crews from both CCC Camps GNP-4 and GNP-5 spent many hours clearing debris along the shore and exposed flats of the reservoir. (*Marion Post Walcott photo, Library of Congress*)

Lake Sherburne sixty years later looks remarkably the same. (*Photo by author, taken August 8, 2001*)

This view of Lake Sherburne is from near the outlet of the lake. CCC boys had to clear a great deal of debris that accumulated in this area from winds blowing down valley toward the dam. The Many Glacier entrance station and Sherburne historic district are visible at right center. (*Photo by author, taken July 29, 2007*)

Lake Sherburne dam and outlet, an area often becoming clogged with debris that required clearance by CCC crews. (*Photo by author, taken August 8, 2001*)

Three C C C Men Drown As Montana Launch Sinks

GLACIER PARK, Mont., July 23 (P)—Four Civilian Conservation Corps workers managed to reach the shore of Lake Sherburne today, when a launch carrying a party of seven men suddenly sank just after the party had taken off from the dock for the opposite shore with lunches for another group of forest workers.

Sherburne lake is 55 miles from here.

The three drowned men were:
M. Greppo Jr., Schenectady, N. Y.
A. Montemarian, Brooklyn, N. Y.
Gilbert Cooper, Ronan, Mont.

The launch had a capacity of 20 passengers and was not overloaded, reports said.

Left: Newspaper clipping describing the tragedy that befell a CCC work crew on Lake Sherburne. (*Salt Lake City Tribune, July 24, 1934, p. 11*)

Below: The down-valley wind can blow hard sometimes across Lake Sherburne, as evidenced by the dust in the air here, which can cause logs and debris to be pushed down-lake towards the dam water intake where CCC boys had to clear it. (*Photo by author, taken August, 1973*)

Many Glacier Campground was cleared, laid out with roads, and planted with acres of trees. Visitors to the Swiftcurrent cabins and nearby campground today likely have no idea that virtually all the trees in those areas are not natural, but were planted by the CCC.[15]

Part of the work in the early days of the CCC was helping clear and maintain roadside edges, prior to those roads being paved. Most park roads including the Many Glacier Road were not paved until just before or after World War II. Gravel roads were susceptible to vegetation encroachment unless constantly cleared every summer. The Many Glacier Road was also susceptible to forest blowdown along Lake Sherburne, and both Camps GNP-4 and GNP-5 spent time every summer during those camps' existence maintaining the vital tourist link from Babb all the way to Swiftcurrent.

As was true elsewhere in Glacier Park, telephone communications were becoming increasingly important in connecting the east to the west side of the park, especially after the opening of Going-to-the-Sun Road in 1933. Modern readers may not be familiar with the single-strand-of-wire telephone lines that typified the 1930s. These wires had to be strung by hand and were an integral part of the communications needed for fire protection and for calling CCC boys to sites for fire suppression. CCC workers from the Swiftcurrent valley camps had to string telephone wire up into the Many Glacier area from Babb, from Babb along the Park boundary southward to St. Mary, and northward to ranger stations between Babb and the Canadian border.

The main building of the Swiftcurrent Motor Inn in the Many Glacier valley was constructed by the CCC. The building is shown here boarded up for the winter. (*Photo by author, taken February 6, 1995*)

A fuller view of the front of the Swiftcurrent Motor Inn, taken September 2, 2013. (*Charles Swaney photo, Creative Commons*)

CCC crews built many of the small "auto cabins" in circular "loop" groups at Swiftcurrent. One such group is shown here in 1941. The effects of the 1936 Heaven's Peak fire are apparent in the burned timber. (*Marion Post Walcott photo, Library of Congress*)

One of the CCC-built "auto cabins" loops at Swiftcurrent by the Many Glacier campground. (*T. J. Hileman photo, National Park Service*)

Loop D cabins built by the CCC at Swiftcurrent, September 3, 2013. (*Charles Swaney photo, Creative Commons*)

The Swiftcurrent showers and laundry facility were also built by the CCC, completed in the fall of 1935. (*Charles Swaney photo, Creative Commons*)

Also at Swiftcurrent, the CCC cleared deadwood from the Heaven's Peak fire and established the Many Glacier campground. (*Charles Swaney photo, Creative Commons*)

Right: Another view of the CCC-constructed Many Glacier campground at Swiftcurrent. (*Charles Swaney photo, Creative Commons*)

Below: CCC boys working on the road between Many Glacier Hotel, seen across Swiftcurrent Lake, and Swiftcurrent tourist facilities, 1938. (*Montana Historical Society photo 34-391*)

Above: Similar view to previous photo almost sixty years later, across frozen Swiftcurrent Lake to the Many Glacier Hotel. (*Photo by author, February 6, 1995*)

Left: CCC workers along the park boundary near Babb install and test a phone line, 1938. (*Glacier National Park*)

CCC Work at St. Mary and Roes Creek (Rising Sun)

Park service facilities in St. Mary were minimal until the opening of Going-to-the-Sun Road in 1933. Once that road was opened, however, it quickly became apparent that having the park's east side headquarters in Glacier Park/East Glacier was a disadvantage because of that village's somewhat isolated location and distance from the new trans-park road. A small ranger station in St. Mary suddenly needed rapid upgrading to serve as the district headquarters for the eastern half of the park. Fortunately, the CCC was available to provide the manpower necessary to accomplish this task.

St. Mary sits at the junction of Going-to-the-Sun Road and U.S. Highway 89, which runs north to the Canadian border and south to Browning. The village of St. Mary is located on the east side of Divide Creek on the Blackfeet Reservation, but the new park district headquarters complex was located on the west side of the creek on Glacier Park land. Prior to 1933, only the old St. Mary Ranger Station—a historical structure built in 1913 with a woodshed, barn, and fencing—served the St. Mary area.[16, 17]

The St. Mary National Park Service complex is a sprawling group of buildings almost completely hidden from tourists on nearby Going-to-the-Sun Road or U.S. Highway 89. Specifically designed to not distract from the natural setting, the area is known in historical preservation parlance as the St. Mary Utility Historic District. Three distinct areas of use, representative of the district's primary functions, are included within the boundaries. These include historic domestic buildings, the maintenance yard where Park Service equipment and equipment repair facilities are housed, and a somewhat removed barn complex (to shelter workers and residents from the "aroma" of horses and mules). A total of eleven buildings from these three use areas were built or upgraded by the CCC. These include the barn, tackroom, and blacksmith shop in the barn complex, a residence and a large dormitory, and several buildings in the maintenance yard including the gas and oil building, three equipment sheds, a paint shop, and a fire cache moved to St. Mary from East Glacier.[18]

The buildings in the barn complex were built in the early years of the CCC. The blacksmith shop, built in 1934, was the first new construction in the barn complex. The barn, built by CCC boys in 1935, is a rustic style similar to the barns built at ranger stations on the west side of the park. The tackroom, originally built as a woodshed, was also built in 1935, although ambiguity exists as to whether it was actually built by the CCC or by the park service.[19]

The maintenance yard occupies the most surface space in the Utility Historic District. The most "historic looking" building is the Gas and Oil House, built in 1938, described by the National Park Service in the following way:

> This building is one of the finest examples of rustic log construction and design in the park. It is an attractive standout from the other, utilitarian buildings in the St. Mary maintenance yard. Its low profile and use of large logs with chopper cut ends give the building a "wilderness" appearance. The covered fueling bay, with its decorative log framing and supports, is also noteworthy. The building's historic setting—

View across Divide Creek to the location, behind the fence in the trees, of the St. Mary Utility Historic District, where most buildings were built by the CCC. (*Photo by author, August 26, 1991*)

The view with rainbow, from the CCC-built dormitory in the St. Mary Ranger Station complex, Singleshot Mountain on the left and East Flattop Mountain on the right. (*Photo by author, August 8, 1995*)

surrounded by asphalt, at the center of the maintenance district—remains virtually unaltered and contributes to the building's historic association with the growth of the park's transportation infrastructure, increased visitation, and commensurate changes in the park's maintenance facilities.[20]

The three equipment sheds in the maintenance yard are largely unremarkable-looking structures appearing much like each other. They are also similar to the equipment sheds we have already seen on the west side in the West Glacier Historic District. Such sheds are vital for storing equipment and vehicles during the harsh Glacier Park winters. All three sheds were constructed by the CCC. The two buildings still used as equipment sheds were built simultaneously in 1936, as single-room buildings with five garage doors and maintenance bays. The third shed, built by the CCC but not specified as to year of construction, serves now as a plumbing and carpenter shop.[21]

The residential structures include a small home built in Glacier Park/East Glacier in 1928 as a fire cache. It was moved by the CCC to St. Mary to ease the chronic housing shortage there in 1934. The large dormitory building was constructed to house as many as 100 people. It was begun with CCC labor in 1939, and CCC work continued on it through 1941. When the CCC was dissolved in the summer of 1942, the building was roughly 75 percent complete. National Park Service crews finished the construction and made it useable after World War II, finally providing adequate housing space for seasonal employees.[22]

In the summer of 1992, I stayed in the St. Mary dorm for two weeks while carrying out research approved by Glacier National Park. The residents of the dorm included seasonal rangers, seasonal ranger-naturalists, trail crew, various Park technicians, as well as an ever-changing array of graduate students and college professors/researchers like myself. The interior of the dorm is not luxurious by any means, but rooms contained bunk beds, a small table and two chairs for meals, a small stove, toilet, and shower. A common room for reading, after-hour drinks, ping-pong games, and conversation was a good place for meeting and deciding whether to cook dinner or go to a restaurant in the village of St. Mary (the restaurants often won out after a hard day of fieldwork in the mountains).

Some 5 miles westward up Going-to-the-Sun Road from St. Mary on the north shore of St. Mary Lake lies the tourist complex known today as Rising Sun (the name "Rising Sun" was not in use until 1950), known in the CCC days as Roes (sometimes spelled Rose) Creek. Recall that a CCC Camp, GNP-11, was established at this location in 1934. CCC Camp GNP-11 was involved in a variety of trail and road-clearing jobs at today's Rising Sun complex and along Going-to-the-Sun Road on the east side. The CCC also cleared and developed what is the present-day Rising Sun Campground, planting trees to provide revegetation and shade as well. Some 74 acres around the campground were also subjected to eradication efforts for white pine blister rust. As the closest camp on either side of the park to Logan Pass, CCC boys from Camp GNP-11 were sent to a spike camp at Logan Pass for work on the trans-park telephone line through Hidden Pass and down into the Avalanche Creek

New oil house in the St. Mary Ranger Station historic district, built by the CCC, 1938. (*Glacier National Park Annual Report, 1938*)

Updates to the CCC-built oil house only slightly mask its historic look. (*National Park Service photo*)

New equipment shed at the St. Mary Ranger Station, built by the CCC in 1938. (*Glacier National Park Annual Report, 1938*)

Dormitory at St. Mary, built by the CCC. This dormitory was one of the largest single structures built anywhere in the park by the CCC. (*National Park Service*)

Aerial view of the setting of the Rising Sun tourist facilities, on the fan-shaped surface at lower left directly above St. Mary Lake. (*Photo by author, August 9, 1995*)

CCC camp on Roes/Rose Creek at current location of Rising Sun camp store and motel shown in a subsequent photo, *c.* 1934. (*National Register of Historic Places*)

CCC crews stationed at Roes Creek carried out road clearance work, such as shown here along Going-to-the Sun Road between Rising Sun and Baring Creek, 1934. (*Glacier National Park Annual Report, 1934*)

valley on the west side of the park. Work on the trans-park telephone line from Logan Pass over Hidden Pass was one of the primary jobs of Camp GNP-11.[23]

A CCC-built camp tender's cabin was planned in May 1935 and completed on September 29, 1937. The building is stylistically a log cabin and looks more similar to park service-constructed cabins built in the 1920s than to most CCC-constructed buildings in the park. This building seems to be the only surviving CCC building at Roes Creek, as the cookhouse structure there built in 1936 was razed after the camp was disbanded around 1939. After Camp GNP-11 was disbanded, planning for use of the space it had occupied began, and in 1941 a new concessionaire-built camp store and auto camp (motel) was built to facilitate the increase in automobile traffic in the park resulting from the opening of Going-to-the-Sun Road and improving economic conditions. The site has good views of the mountain peaks of the St. Mary valley and is adjacent to the campground cleared and developed by the CCC.

This camp tender's cabin at Rising Sun was constructed by the CCC and completed in September 1937. (*National Park Service*)

The Rising Sun camp store, motel, and parking lot, built in 1941, were constructed at the location of the former CCC Camp GNP-11. (*Photo by author, August 6, 1996*)

Scenic setting of Rising Sun on St. Mary Lake. CCC structures were distributed throughout the area, but only the camp tender's cabin remains. (*Photo by author, August 6, 1996*)

CCC Work in the Cut Bank and Two Medicine Valleys

Southward of St. Mary, the next road penetrating into Glacier Park is the five-mile-long primitive gravel road leading from U.S. Highway 89 to the Cut Bank campground and ranger station. The ranger station predates the CCC era, having been constructed in 1917. Behind the ranger station is a barn and woodshed built in 1935 by the CCC (information on which CCC camp supplied the labor for this work is not available, but could have been from either the camp at Two Medicine to the south or the camp at Roes Creek).

The barn at Cut Bank is considered "among Glacier's finest examples of exaggerated rustic design." The barn is a "one-and-one-half story rectangular building constructed of saddle-notched logs with chopper-cut ends." The nearby woodshed is a "fine example of NPS modified rustic architecture," with exposed exterior log framing. Both the barn and woodshed appear to be unmodified from CCC days.[24]

The Two Medicine valley entrance into Glacier Park, about 21 miles south of the Cut Bank complex, is reached via U.S. Highway 89 to Kiowa, then southward on Montana Highway 49 to the turnoff into the valley. From the turn-off, it is about 4 miles along the north shore of Lower Two Medicine Lake to the park boundary and entrance station. CCC Camp GNP-6 was established on the north shore of the lake in 1933. That camp was apparently only in existence for two years, through 1934, according to reports from Glacier Park Superintendent E. T. Scoyen. The camp was reported to have been razed and the grounds "re-naturalized" by the CCC in Superintendent Scoyen's annual report for 1938.[25]

Above: The Cut Bank valley and ranger station, between St. Mary and Two Medicine, is the least-visited such station on the east side of Glacier Park. The ranger station and associated outbuildings were built in the clearing roughly in the center of the picture. (*Fred H. Kiser, Oregon Historical Society Library ba020876*)

Left: The CCC built the barn and woodshed at the Cut Bank Ranger Station in 1935. The front of the shed is shown here to the rear of the ranger station that pre-dates the CCC. (*National Register of Historic Places*)

The CCC-built Cut Bank Ranger Station barn, seen from the side and rear. (*National Park Service*)

CCC work in the Two Medicine valley was concentrated around two primary goals—working with the CCC-ID in keeping Lower Two Medicine Lake and the water intake system of the dam impounding the lake free of floating woody debris, and attempting to eradicate white pine blister rust that affected the five-needle pine trees at upper elevations in the valley. The boys of Camp GNP-6 also carried out roadside clearance and clean-up along the entrance road into the valley, which like the other two goals was an ongoing project. They additionally landscaped and cleaned up the Two Medicine Campground.

As Lower Two Medicine Lake is a reservoir in which the water is drawn down for irrigation purposes over the course of the summer and into early autumn, large areas of the lake become exposed mudflats in late summer. This irrigation drawdown of the lake exposes woody debris needing clean-up, and the unsightly mudflats were a point of contention between Glacier Park and the Blackfeet Reservation, which used the irrigation water. The written exchanges between the two agencies were at times harsh and do not reflect the apparent cooperation that existed between the two groups of CCC/CCC-ID workers attempting to keep the woody debris clear.[26]

White pine blister rust eradication was the other major focus in the Two Medicine valley for CCC labor. This work continued well after the closure of Camp GNP-6, and it is unclear from the park superintendent reports which CCC camp(s) supplied the labor for this work after the local camp closure. The park carried out a preliminary survey for white pine blister rust in the fall of 1938, and eradication attempts began in earnest in 1939. The Two Medicine valley is mentioned in all superintendent reports from 1939 onward as being one of the major areas in which CCC eradication efforts were carried out. The superintendent report for 1941, as an example, states that 120 acres in the Two Medicine valley were subjected to blister rust eradication efforts.[27]

Lower Two Medicine Lake, a reservoir seen here looking south across the lake to Scenic Point, straddles the Glacier Park/Blackfeet Reservation border. Workers from both the CCC and the CCC-ID worked to keep the reservoir and dam intake clear of woody debris. (*Photo by author, September 15, 2005*)

CCC boys on clean-up work on the entrance road to Two Medicine, on the north side of Lower Two Medicine Lake, seen at upper right. (*George A. Grant photo, Glacier National Park Grant 855*)

White pine blister rust is a fungus that enters white pine trees through their needles. Once inside the tree, the fungus spreads down the trunk and eventually girdles the tree, killing it. If the girdling does not kill the host tree, complete defoliation eventually does. The first signs of an infection in a tree do not show up for three years after infestation. One characteristic of the fungus that makes the eradication of white pine blister rust easy is the fungus' particular life cycle. The rust needs an alternate host for incubation of the spores that attack the pines. Bushes of the genus *Ribes*, gooseberries and currents, are the only suitable alternate hosts for this fungus. Therefore, elimination of *Ribes* bushes in an area makes the white pines in that area safe from white pine blister rust.[28]

The CCC used two methods in Glacier Park in an attempt to eradicate the host *Ribes* (none of which are employed today—the National Park Service no longer attempts artificial removal of *Ribes*, allowing the blister rust to run its course as a natural ecological process). These included pulling the bush by hand or with the assistance of a grubbing tool, or spraying the plant with salt mixtures or diesel oil (a method that was used in the Two Medicine valley) carried in a backpack-mounted pump.[29]

This hand-colored photograph shows CCC boys high on the flank of Rising Wolf Mountain in the Two Medicine valley, pulling *Ribes* plants in an attempt to eradicate the spread of white pine blister rust, *c.* 1938. (*National Museum of Forest Service History*)

The CCC and CCC-ID at Glacier Park Station

As the Glacier National Park district headquarters for the east side of the park until 1933, Glacier Park Station (East Glacier) had the awkward geography of being located not in the park but on the Blackfeet Reservation. Thus, the park service facilities were physically as well as culturally separate from the residents of Glacier Park Station. The district office and buildings were, and still are, located north of Glacier Park Lodge along Montana Highway 49, largely removed from the main residential section of the village along and east of U.S. Highway 2.

By the CCC era, and coincident with the opening of Going-to-the-Sun Road and transference of the park service district offices to St. Mary, many of the early twentieth-century buildings in the Glacier Park Station park service complex had become old and dilapidated. In 1937, the CCC razed four such buildings—an equipment shed, a bunkhouse/mess hall, a warehouse, and storage/garage—and salvaged usable lumber. Also recall that a residential building had been removed from the complex in 1934 and moved to St. Mary to alleviate the housing shortage there.[30]

The village library and community hall for the village of Glacier Park Station/ East Glacier is located on the north end of town on the east side of U.S. Highway 2. The building attracts little attention from tourists on Highway 2 anxious to get to Glacier National Park, but it is definitely worth taking a few minutes to examine the historical and architectural aspects of the structure. The Glacier Park Woman's Club acquired the land on which the building is located from the Great Northern Railway in 1928. In 1933, the club donated the land to Glacier County, in which Glacier Park Station is located, in order for the local CCC-ID labor force to build a structure for the county that could house a library and serve as a community hall. The building is a saddle-notched example of CCC Rustic architecture. After completion, Glacier County donated the building and land back to the Glacier Park Woman's Club, and the building is now on the National Register of Historic Places.[31]

View of East Glacier (known then as Midvale) Ranger Station complex, 1935. CCC work here was largely focused on demolishing dilapidated buildings from the early twentieth century. (*Lester M. Moe photo, U.S. Geological Survey*)

Glacier Park Woman's Club, East Glacier. Built by the CCC-ID on land donated by the Woman's Club to Glacier County in 1933, it is located at the intersection of U.S. 2 and Glacier Avenue, on the right when traveling toward Browning from East Glacier. (*Montana State Historic Preservation Office*)

Above: Side view of the CCC-ID constructed Glacier Park Woman's Club, which serves as the village library and community hall. (*Montana State Historic Preservation Office*)

Right: Historical marker providing background information on the Glacier Park Woman's Club. (*Barry Swackhamer photo, HMdb.org*)

The Presidential Visit of FDR

August 5, 1934, was a date of extreme significance for Glacier National Park and the CCC. On that day, "[t]he most important event in Glacier National Park History" took place—a presidential visit by President Franklin D. Roosevelt (FDR) and a party including First Lady Eleanor Roosevelt and Secretary of the Interior Harold Ickes. The purpose of the visit was to showcase America's National Parks and the role of the CCC in improving park facilities across the country. The significance of this visit is underscored by the fact that this was the first time an American president had ever entered Glacier National Park. These complementary goals were accomplished by a day-long visit across both sides of Glacier Park, followed in the evening by FDR giving a radio speech about the importance of the CCC from the Two Medicine Chalets near East Glacier.[1]

FDR's presidential visit to Glacier Park began on a Sunday morning, arriving by a special Great Northern Railway train from Portland, Oregon. After disembarking at Belton Station at the west entrance to Going-to-the-Sun Road (in what is now known as West Glacier), the presidential party entered open touring cars for the trip across the Continental Divide. From Belton, the tour party proceeded to Apgar along a road lined with cheering CCC boys from the westside camps, and then along the shore of Lake McDonald and up the McDonald Creek valley. Climbing the Garden Wall, the party reached the high point, Logan Pass, where a short stop was made. From Logan Pass, they proceeded down the east side of the park to a stop at CCC camp GNP-11 at Roes/Rose Creek (Rising Sun). A planned stop at Sun Point had to be skipped because of time constraints.[2]

Following the stop at the CCC camp, the presidential party drove northward to Babb and headed west up the Swiftcurrent valley to the Many Glacier Hotel, where lunch was served. After lunch, the group visited CCC camp GNP-4, where the president made a strong impression on one observer. Bill Briggs, a member of CCC Company 1240 at camp GNP-4, wrote:

> I saw the President! For eleven minutes he was with us; blue-eyed, genial, smiling
> ... his keen eyes flashing over our camp and over us. I found a giant with massive

President Franklin Roosevelt in a Glacier Park Transport Company touring car, during his visit to Glacier National Park on August 5, 1934. (*FDR Presidential Library* OF 466)

FDR and touring car group at Logan Pass, having come up Going-to-the-Sun Road from Lake McDonald. (*Glacier National Park*)

Similar view as in previous photo, looking northward to the Garden Wall from Logan Pass. (*Photo by author, July 30, 2009*)

shoulders and powerful arms that belied the steel braces on his legs. His face was ruddy and deeply tanned, his blue eyes flashed vigor and good humor, and his shock of iron-gray hair tossed in the wind. He spoke quietly … heartily … everything about him spoke of power. Even the surrounding mountains and green-clad pines must have sensed that a great man was in our midst. Never did they seem so majestic and grand. The air was electric with the sense of a great happening.[3]

The presidential party subsequently drove back out to Babb and headed southward on the Blackfeet Highway (U.S. Highway 89 and Montana Route 49) to the entrance to the Two Medicine valley in Glacier Park. The party arrived at the Two Medicine Chalets on the shore of Two Medicine Lake at 5.45 p.m. local time. Both the Many Glacier and Two Medicine roads had been repaired and oiled for the visit.[4]

At the Two Medicine Chalets, the presidential party was met by a group of about forty CCC workers comprising a chorus. The CCC chorus sang several songs, including favorites of the president. Also greeting the president and his party was a group of about forty Blackfeet Indians in full traditional regalia. The president, Mrs. Roosevelt, and Secretary of the Interior Ickes were adopted as members of the Blackfeet tribe in an induction ceremony with presentation of gifts, including a ceremonial headdress and peace pipe for President Roosevelt. The president was given the Blackfeet name "Lone Chief," Mrs. Roosevelt was named "Medicine Pipe Woman" and "Grand White Mother," and Secretary Ickes was named "Big Bear." Following the induction ceremony, the Blackfeet contingent presented a number of their traditional tribal dances.

Above left: FDR party leaving Many Glacier Hotel (out of sight on right) after lunch stop, August 5, 1934. (*Glacier National Park Annual Report, 1935*)

Above right: Blackfeet tipis at Two Medicine, awaiting arrival of President Roosevelt. (*Montana Historical Society 955-525*)

FDR and traveling party arrive at Two Medicine chalets. A chorus of CCC workers provided a vocal program upon arrival of the presidential party. (*FDR Presidential Library NPx # 03-24*)

Above left: FDR and party listen to a presentation by Blackfeet elders on the shore of Two Medicine Lake in front of the main building of the Two Medicine Chalets, with Sinopah Mountain in the background across the lake. FDR, Eleanor Roosevelt (second from right), and Secretary of the Interior Harold Ickes were adopted into the Blackfeet tribe. (*Associated Press*)

Above right: FDR and Secretary Ickes after the president received a ceremonial headdress and a peace pipe from the Blackfeet as part of their adoption into the tribe. (*Associated Press*)

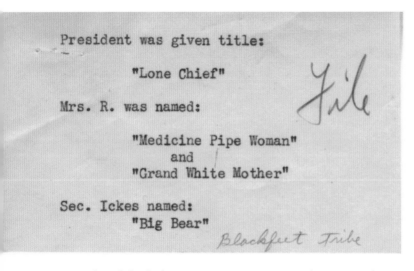
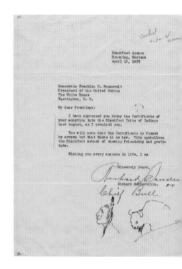

Above left: The honorary names given to President Roosevelt, Mrs. Roosevelt, and Secretary Ickes as certified in a part of a letter from the Blackfeet tribe. (*FDR Library, Marist University PPF 2397*)

Above right: Letter sent to President Roosevelt from Chief Bull (Richard Sanderville) the following spring, accompanying the official Certificate of Adoption for FDR. (*FDR Library, Marist University PPF 2397*)

After the welcome and adoption ceremony, President Roosevelt and party adjourned to the main building of the Two Medicine Chalets, to prepare for FDR's forthcoming radio address to the nation. At 7.30 p.m. Mountain Standard Time, the president delivered his nationwide radio broadcast from a room fronting on Two Medicine Lake. In his speech, he praised the outstanding scenery of Glacier National Park and the idea of national parks. He also specifically addressed the work of the CCC (known as one of his favorite New Deal programs), stating:

Today I have seen some of the work of the Civilian Conservation Corps boys in this Northwestern country. Of the three hundred thousand young men in these Camps, 75,000 are at work in our national parks. Here, under trained leadership, we are helping these men to help themselves and their families and at the same time we are making the parks more available and more useful for the average citizen. Hundreds of miles of firebreaks have been built, fire hazards have been reduced on great tracts of timberland, thousands of miles of roadside have been cleared, 2,500 miles of trails have been constructed and 10,000 acres have been reforested. Other tens of thousands of acres have been treated for tree disease and soil erosion. This is but another example of our efforts to build not for today alone, but for tomorrow as well.[5]

After finishing his radio address, the president and his party decided to move on to Glacier Park rather than spend the night as originally planned in rooms at Two Medicine, and the group proceeded on to Glacier Park Lodge for a brief reception, after which the group boarded the special presidential train at Glacier Park Station at 9.30 p.m. After spending the night aboard the train, the group left the next morning at 8 a.m., August 6, heading eastward across Montana and toward Washington, D.C.[6]

In 2009, the seventh-fifth anniversary of FDR's visit to Glacier National Park was commemorated with a reconstruction of his ride through the park, with his great-granddaughter, Kate Roosevelt, as one of the participants. The same 1927 Glacier Park Transport Company Cadillac that was used by FDR in 1934 was used in the reconstruction. In total, the reconstructed ride used three 1927 Cadillacs and a 1925 White Motor Company bus. The original presidential ride in 1934 used seven 1927 Cadillacs.[7]

Above: View of the Two Medicine Chalets, on the far shore of Two Medicine Lake, the site of the tribal induction ceremony. (*George A. Grant photo, Glacier National Park GLAC 11335*)

Below left: The main Two Medicine Chalet, today the only remaining building that serves as the Two Medicine Campstore, in 1930. (*T. J. Hileman photo, Glacier National Park GLAC 10166*)

Below right: More recent view of the Two Medicine Campstore similar to the 1930 view in previous picture. Rising Wolf Mountain dominates the view to the rear. (*Photo by author, July 21, 2012*)

Right: A page from the text of the radio speech in support of the CCC delivered from the Two Medicine Chalet main building by President Roosevelt, August 5, 1934. (*U.S. National Archives*)

Below: Group gathered at Glacier Park Lodge in East Glacier awaiting FDR's arrival from Two Medicine. (*Montana Historical Society*)

- 2 -

large tract of parched land for the benefit of this and future generations. Many families in the days to come, I am confident, will thank us of this generation for providing small farms on which they will at least be able to make an honest and honorable livelihood.

Today, for the first time in my life, I have seen Glacier Park. Perhaps I can best express to you my thrill and delight by saying that I wish every American, old and young, could have been with me today. The great mountains, the glaciers, the lakes and the trees make me long to stay here for all the rest of the summer.

Comparisons are generally objectionable and yet it is not unkind to say from the standpoint of scenery alone that if many and indeed most of our American national parks were to be set down anywhere on the continent of Europe thousands of Americans would journey all the way across the ocean in order to see their beauties.

There is nothing so American as our national parks. The scenery and wild life are native and the fundamental idea behind the parks is native. It is, in brief, that the country belongs to the people; that what it is and what it is in the process of making is for the enrichment of the lives of all of us. Thus the parks stand as the outward symbol of this great human principle.

It was on a famous night, sixty-four years ago, that a group of men who had been exploring the Yellowstone

Glacier Park Lodge as viewed from Glacier Park Station in East Glacier, 2012. (*Photo by author, July 21, 2012*)

Looking toward Glacier Park Station from Glacier Park Lodge, this is a view similar to what the presidential greeting party would have seen looking across the lodge lawn to the railroad station in 1934. (*Photo by author, July 21, 2012*)

AFTERWORD

The Lasting Legacy of FDR's CCC in Glacier National Park

It has been eighty years since the CCC left Glacier National Park. For today's visitors, did the CCC produce a legacy that still matters? Of course. Every visitor who enters the park at West Glacier passes through the entrance station built by the CCC. If visitors take a side-trip into the Park Headquarters complex, roughly half of the buildings they encounter are CCC structures. Entering the park at St. Mary, much of the district headquarters there is a result of the CCC. Most of the campground structures built along Going-to-the-Sun Road and at campgrounds along all the other park roads were built by the CCC. Trails were built and maintained by the CCC, some of which are still hiked today, even though many of the CCC fire trails have fallen into disuse.

The CCC legacy of firefighting is more subtle to see, because in the eighty-plus years since CCC boys risked their lives to save park forests, burned areas have regrown—not to the full maturity of some park forests, but enough so that the average park visitor does not notice the difference. Similarly, the snag-removal of burned trees carried out over thousands of acres is not noticed.

Nonetheless, Glacier National Park looks much like it does today thanks to the wisdom of Franklin Delano Roosevelt in conceptualizing the CCC, thanks to the United States Congress for passing the legislation creating the CCC, thanks to the untold hours of effort put into improving and protecting this truly great American national park by the U.S. Army that managed the camps, the National Park Service that oversaw the work, and most of all thanks to the toil and sweat of the boys of the Civilian Conservation Corps.

Endnotes

Chapter 1

1 Hanson, J. A., *The Civilian Conservation Corps in the Northern Rocky Mountains* (Laramie, WY: Department of History, University of Wyoming, 1973), p. 1.
2 Pearson, P. O., *Fighting for the Forest: How FDR's Civilian Conservation Corps Helped Save America* (New York, NY: Simon & Schuster, 2019), p. 62.
3 Paige, J. C., *The Civilian Conservation Corps and the National Park Service, 1933–1942—An Administrative History* (Washington, D.C.: National Park Service, Department of the Interior, 1985), p. 8.
4 *Ibid.*, p. 11.
5 Montana Historical Society, *Land of Many Stories—The People & Histories of Glacier National Park* (Helena, MT: Montana Historical Society, no date given), p. 81.
6 Alexander, B. F., *The New Deal's Forest Army: How the Civilian Conservation Corps Worked* (Baltimore, MD: Johns Hopkins University Press, 2018), p. 106.
7 Paige, *op. cit.*, p. 12.
8 *Ibid.*
9 *Ibid.*, p. 15.
10 Redinger, M. A., *The Civilian Conservation Corps as a Tool of the National Park Service: The Development of Glacier and Yellowstone National Parks, 1933–1942* (Missoula, MT: Graduate School, University of Montana, 1988), p. 101.
11 Ober, M. J., 'The CCC Experience in Glacier National Park', *Montana the Magazine of Western History*, vol. 26 no. 3 (Helena, MT: Montana Historical Society, 1976), p. 32.

Chapter 2

1 Ober, M. J., 'The CCC Experience in Glacier National Park', *Montana the Magazine of Western History*, vol. 26 no. 3, p. 32.
2 Sharp, B., *The Civilian Conservation Corps in Montana and under the Fort Missoula C.C.C. District—May, 1933 through July, 1942* (Bozeman, MT: self-published, 1988), pp. 2–4.
3 *Ibid.*, p. 6.
4 Ober, *op. cit.*, p. 34.
5 Redinger, M. A., *The Civilian Conservation Corps as a Tool of the National Park Service: The Development of Glacier and Yellowstone National Parks, 1933–1942*, p. 61.
6 Scoyen, E. T., *Glacier National Park Annual Report, Fiscal Year 1934* (West Glacier, MT: Glacier National Park, 1934), p. 9.

7 Ober, *op. cit.*, p. 34.

8 Hanson, J. A., *The Civilian Conservation Corps in the Northern Rocky Mountains*, p. 390.

9 Scoyen, E. T., *Glacier National Park Annual Report, Fiscal Year 1936* (West Glacier, MT: Glacier National Park, 1936), p. 20.

10 Park Superintendents E. T. Scoyen and D. S. Libbey, *Glacier National Park Annual Reports, Fiscal Years 1937–1943* (West Glacier, MT: Glacier National Park), various pages.

11 Redinger, *op. cit.*, p. 101.

12 Brott, J. H., *Annual Forestry Report, Blackfeet Agency* (Browning, MT: Blackfeet Agency, Indian Field Service, U.S. Department of the Interior, 1934), p. 13.

13 Montana Historical Society, *Land of Many Stories—The People & Histories of Glacier National Park*, p. 81.

Chapter 3

1 Ober, M. J., 'The CCC Experience in Glacier National Park', *Montana the Magazine of Western History*, vol. 26 no. 3, p. 33.

2 Hanson, J. A., *The Civilian Conservation Corps in the Northern Rocky Mountains*, p. 104.

3 *Ibid.*, p. 119.

4 *Ibid.*, p. 5.

5 Sharp, M. I., 'Civilian Conservation Corps in Montana: 1933–1942', *The Western Planner*, vol. 37 no. 4 (Cheyenne, WY: Western Planning Resources, Inc., 2016), p. 3.

6 Hanson, *op. cit.*, pp. 77–79.

7 Smith, *op. cit.*, p. 10.

8 *Glacier Ice Sheet* (Glacier National Park, MT: Camps GNP-4 and GNP-13, August, 1935), p. 12.

9 Green, C., *Montana Memories Vol. IV* (Great Falls, MT: Blue Print & Letter Co., 1972), pp. 65–66.

10 Mooney, T., 'Mascot', *Glacial Drift*, vol. 7 no. 3, (Belton, MT: Glacier National Park, 1934), p. 29.

11 Fladmark, E., "At Anaconda Camp", *Glacial Drift*, vol. 6 no. 3, (Belton, MT: Glacier National Park, 1933), p. 3.

12 Hanson, *op. cit.*, p. 173.

13 Redinger, M. A., *The Civilian Conservation Corps as a Tool of the National Park Service: The Development of Glacier and Yellowstone National Parks, 1933–1942*, pp. 23–24.

14 *Glacier Ice Sheet* (Glacier National Park, MT: Camps GNP-4 and GNP-13, September 1, 1935), p. 4.

15 *Babb Gazette* (Glacier National Park, MT: Camp GNP-13, June-July 1936), p. 2.

16 *Ibid.*, p. 7.

17 *Belton Beacon* (Glacier National Park, MT: Camp GNP-1, September 1936), p. 1.

18 *Glacier Ice Sheet* (Glacier National Park, MT: Camps GNP-4 and GNP-13, September 15, 1935), p. 6.

19 Green, *op. cit.*, p. 36.

20 *Babb Echo* (Glacier National Park, MT: Camps GNP-4 and GNP-13, July 31, 1936), p. 4.

21 Hanson, *op. cit.*, p. 194.

Chapter 4

1 Minetor, R., *Historic Glacier National Park: The Stories Behind One of America's Great Treasures* (Guilford, CT: Lyons Press, 2016), pp. 140–141.

2 Scoyen, E. T., *Glacier National Park Annual Report, Fiscal Year 1933* (West Glacier, MT: Glacier National Park, 1933), pp. 17–18.

3 Libbey, D. S., *Glacier National Park Annual Report, Fiscal Year 1941* (West Glacier, MT: Glacier National Park, 1941), p. 12.

4 *Ibid.*, p. 5.

5 Libbey, D. S., *Glacier National Park Annual Report, Fiscal Year 1942* (West Glacier, MT: Glacier National Park, 1942), p. 5.

6 Libbey, D. S., *Glacier National Park Annual Report, Fiscal Year 1940* (West Glacier, MT: Glacier National Park, 1940), p. 5.

7 Moravek, V., *It Happened in Glacier National Park* (Guilford, CT: Globe Pequot Press, 2005), p. 51.

8 Shaw, C., *The Flathead Story* (Kalispell, MT: Flathead National Forest, U.S. D.A. Forest Service, 1967), p. 25.

9 Larson, R. L., *Firestorm! The Explosive Heaven's Peak Forest Fire of 1936* (Minneapolis, MN: Glacier Park Foundation, 1987), pp. 10–12.

10 Moravek, *op. cit.*, p. 52.

11 Larson, *op. cit.*, pp. 21–23.

12 McLaughlin, W., *Holocaust! The Night the Fire Crossed Over Swiftcurrent Pass in Glacier National Park* (Self-published, 1978), p. 20.

13 Butler, D. R., *Fire Lookouts of Glacier National Park* (Charleston, SC: Arcadia Publishing, 2014), p. 53.

14 Green, C., *Montana Memories Vol. I—Homesteaders—Forest Fires—Bear Stories* (Great Falls, MT: Thomas Printing, 1969), p. 48.

15 Green, C., *Montana Memories Vol. IV* (Great Falls, MT: Blue Print & Letter Co., 1972), pp. 64–65.

16 Green, 1969 *op. cit.*, p. 49.

17 *Ibid.*, p. 52.

18 Green, 1972 *op. cit.*, pp. 45–46.

Chapter 5

1 Butler, D. R., *Fire Lookouts of Glacier National Park*, p. 18.

2 Ober, M. J., 'The CCC Experience in Glacier National Park', *Montana the Magazine of Western History*, vol. 26 no. 3, p. 35.

3 Redinger, M. A., *The Civilian Conservation Corps as a Tool of the National Park Service: The Development of Glacier and Yellowstone National Parks, 1933–1942*, p. 101.

4 Sharp, B., *The Civilian Conservation Corps in Montana and under the Fort Missoula C.C.C. District—May, 1933 through July, 1942* (Bozeman, MT: self-published, 1988), p. 8.

5 Sharp, B., *Civilian Conservation Corps Casualty List for Montana—April, 1933 to August, 1942* (Bozeman, MT: unpublished typescript, 1987), p. 2.

6 Redinger, *op. cit.*, p. 76.

7 *Ibid.*, p. 77.

8 *Ibid.*, p. 77.

9 Scoyen, E. T., *Glacier National Park Annual Report, Fiscal Year 1933*, p. 18.

10 Scoyen, E. T., *Glacier National Park Annual Report, Fiscal Year 1935* (West Glacier, MT: Glacier National Park, 1935), p. 13.

11 Libbey, D. S., *Glacier National Park Annual Report, Fiscal Year 1941*, page unnumbered.

12 Green, C., *Montana Memories Vol. IV*, pp. 57–58.

13 Rocky Mountains Cooperative Ecosystem Studies Unit, *Glacier National Park Headquarters Historic District Landscape History and Significance Statement* (Santa Fe, NM: National Park Service—Intermountain Region, 2011), p. 15.

14 *Ibid.*, pp. 14–15.

15 *Ibid.*, pp. 13–14.

16 Scoyen, E. T., *Glacier National Park Annual Report, Fiscal Year 1934*, p. 16.

17 Scoyen, E. T., *Glacier National Park Annual Report, Fiscal Year 1938* (West Glacier, MT: Glacier National Park, 1938), p. 22.

18 Libbey 1941, *op. cit.*, p. 6.

19 Scoyen 1935, *op. cit.*, p. 13.

20 Libbey, D. S., *Glacier National Park Annual Report, Fiscal Year 1939* (West Glacier, MT: Glacier National Park, 1939), p. 3.

21 Libbey, D. S., *Glacier National Park Annual Report, Fiscal Year 1940*, p. 7.

22 *Ibid.*, p. 3.

23 National Park Service, *Lake McDonald Lodge Historic District* (Washington, D.C.: National Park Service, 1977), p. 60.

24 Butler, *op. cit.*, p. 34.

25 Hanson, J. A., *The Civilian Conservation Corps in the Northern Rocky Mountains*, p. 272.

26 Guthrie, C. W., D. Fagre, and A. Fagre, *Death & Survival in Glacier National Park* (Helena, MT: Farcountry Press, 2017), p. 291.

27 Minetor, R., *Death in Glacier National Park—Stories of Accidents and Foolhardiness in the Crown of the Continent* (Guilford, CT: Lyons Press, 2016), pp. 44–45.

Chapter 6

1 Scoyen, E. T., *Glacier National Park Annual Report, Fiscal Year 1933*, p. 12.

2 Libbey, D. S., *Glacier National Park Annual Report, Fiscal Year 1939*, p. 7.

3 Ober, M. J., 'The CCC Experience in Glacier National Park', *Montana the Magazine of Western History*, vol. 26 no. 3, p. 35.

4 Redinger, M. A., *The Civilian Conservation Corps as a Tool of the National Park Service: The Development of Glacier and Yellowstone National Parks, 1933–1942*, pp. 66–67.

Chapter 7

1 Butler, D. R., *Fire Lookouts of Glacier National Park*, p. 71.

2 Pulkai, J. S., *Glacier Ice Sheet* (Many Glacier, MT: Civilian Conservation Corps Companies 529 and 593, 1934), p. 5.

3 Butler, *op. cit.*, p. 83.

4 Butler, *op. cit.*, p. 71.

5 Butler, *op. cit.*, p. 62.

6 Sherfy, M., *Red Eagle Lookout Tower Glacier National Park* (Helena, MT: Montana Historical Society, Historical Preservation Office, 1984), p. 3.

7 Butler, *op. cit.*, p. 92.

8 Butler, *op. cit.*, p. 93.

9 Blackfeet Agency, *62137-1934 Blackfeet File No. 339* (Browning, MT: Blackfeet Indian Agency and National Archives and Records Administration, 1934), p. 6.

10 Minetor, R., 2016b, *op. cit.*, p. 133.

11 Cohen, S., *The Tree Army: A Pictorial History of the Civilian Conservation Corps, 1933-1942* (Missoula, MT: Mountain Press Publishing Company, 2018), p. 98.

12 Associated Press, *Three CCC Men Drown as Montana Launch Sinks* (Salt Lake City, UT: Salt Lake City Tribune, 1934), p. 11.

13 Sharp, B., *Civilian Conservation Corps Casualty List for Montana—April, 1933 to August, 1942*, no page number given.

14 Scoyen, E. T., *Glacier National Park Annual Report, Fiscal Year 1933*, p. 17.

15 Scoyen, E. T., *Glacier National Park Annual Report, Fiscal Year 1936*, p. 21.

16 Geoghegan, H., *Historic Structure Report: Old St. Mary Ranger District* (West Glacier, MT: Glacier National Park, 1978), p. 1.

17 National Park Service, *St. Mary Utility Area Historic District* (Washington, D.C.: National Park Service, 1995), p. 3.

18 *Ibid.*, p. 15.

19 *Ibid.*, p. 18.
20 *Ibid.*, p. 14.
21 *Ibid.*, p. 14.
22 *Ibid.*, p. 13.
23 Ober, M. J., 'The CCC Experience in Glacier National Park', *Montana the Magazine of Western History*, vol. 26 no. 3, p. 39.
24 National Park Service, *Cut Bank Ranger Station Historic District* (Washington, D.C.: National Park Service, 1995), p. 3.
25 Scoyen, E. T., *Glacier National Park Annual Report, Fiscal Year 1938*, p. 23.
26 Blackfeet Agency, *DCI 341, Year 1936, File 9085-Part S* (Browning, MT: Blackfeet Indian Agency and National Archives and Records Administration, 1936), no page number given.
27 Libbey, D. S., *Glacier National Park Annual Report, Fiscal Year 1941* (West Glacier, MT: Glacier National Park, 1941), p. 6.
28 Redinger, M. A., *The Civilian Conservation Corps as a Tool of the National Park Service: The Development of Glacier and Yellowstone National Parks, 1933–1942*, p. 62.
29 *Ibid.*, p. 63.
30 National Park Service, *East Glacier Ranger Station Historic District* (Washington, D.C.: National Park Service, 1995), p. 4.
31 Montana National Register Sign Program, *Glacier Park Women's Club* (Helena, MT: Montana Historical Society), accessed June 29, 2021, https://historicmt.org/items/show/2817.

Chapter 8

1 Scoyen, E. T., *Glacier National Park Annual Report, Fiscal Year 1935*, p. 1.
2 Montana Historical Society, *Land of Many Stories—The People & Histories of Glacier National Park*, p. 81.
3 Cornebise, A. E., *The CCC Chronicles: Camp Newspapers of the Civilian Conservation Corps, 1933-1942* (Jefferson, NC: McFarland & Company, Inc., 2004), p. 105.
4 Djuff, R., and C. Morrison, *Waterton and Glacier in a Snap!* (Calgary, Alberta: Rocky Mountain Books, 2005), p. 100.
5 Roosevelt, F. D., *Speech made at Glacier National Park—August 5, 1934.* fdrlibrary.marist.edu/_resources/images/msf/msf00744
6 Djuff and Morrison, *op. cit.*, p. 100.
7 *Cut Bank Pioneer Press, Kate Roosevelt retraces FDR's Glacier visit on 75th anniversary* (Cut Bank, MT: Cut Bank Pioneer Press, August 19, 2009).

Bibliography

Alexander, B.F., *The New Deal's Forest Army: How the Civilian Conservation Corps Worked* (Baltimore, MD: Johns Hopkins University Press, 2018)

Butler, D. R., *Images of America: Fire Lookouts of Glacier National Park* (Charleston, SC: Arcadia Publishing, 2014)

Cohen, S., *The Tree Army: A Pictorial History of the Civilian Conservation Corps, 1933-1942* (Missoula, MT: Mountain Press Publishing Company, 2018)

Cornebise, A. E., *The CCC Chronicles: Camp Newspapers of the Civilian Conservation Corps, 1933-1942* (Jefferson, NC: McFarland & Company, Inc., 2004)

Cut Bank Pioneer Press, Kate Roosevelt retraces FDR's Glacier visit on 75th anniversary (Cut Bank, MT: Cut Bank Pioneer Press, August 19, 2009)

Djuff, R., and C. Morrison, *Waterton and Glacier in a Snap!* (Calgary, Alberta: Rocky Mountain Books, 2005)

Geoghegan, H., *Historic Structure Report: Old St. Mary Ranger District* (West Glacier, MT: Glacier National Park), p. 1.

Green, C., *Montana Memories Vol. I – Homesteaders – Forest Fires – Bear Stories* (Great Falls, MT: Thomas Printing, 1969)

Green, C., *Montana Memories Vol. IV* (Great Falls, MT: Blue Print & Letter Co., 1972)

Guthrie, C. W., D. Fagre, and A. Fagre, *Death & Survival in Glacier National Park* (Helena, MT: Farcountry Press, 2017)

Hanson, J. A., *The Civilian Conservation Corps in the Northern Rocky Mountains* (Laramie, WY: Department of History, University of Wyoming, 1973)

Larson, R. L., *Firestorm! The Explosive Heaven's Peak Forest Fire of 1936* (Minneapolis, MN: Glacier Park Foundation, 1987)

Libbey, D. S., *Glacier National Park Annual Report, Fiscal Year 1939* (West Glacier, MT: Glacier National Park, 1939)

Libbey, D. S., *Glacier National Park Annual Report, Fiscal Year 1940* (West Glacier, MT: Glacier National Park, 1940)

Libbey, D. S., *Glacier National Park Annual Report, Fiscal Year 1941* (West Glacier, MT: Glacier National Park, 1941)

Libbey, D. S., *Glacier National Park Annual Report, Fiscal Year 1942* (West Glacier, MT: Glacier National Park, 1942)

Libbey, D. S., *Glacier National Park Annual Report, Fiscal Year 1943* (West Glacier, MT: Glacier National Park, 1943)

McLaughlin, W., *Holocaust! The Night the Fire Crossed Over Swiftcurrent Pass in Glacier National Park* (Self-published, 1978)

Minetor, R., *Death in Glacier National Park – Stories of Accidents and Foolhardiness in the Crown of the Continent* (Guilford, CT: Lyons Press, 2016a)

Minetor, R., *Historic Glacier National Park: The Stories Behind One of America's Great Treasures* (Guilford, CT: Lyons Press, 2016b)

Montana National Register Sign Program, *Glacier Park Woman's Club* (Helena, MT: Montana Historical Society), accessed June 29, 2021, https://historicmt.org/items/show/2817

Moravek, V., *It Happened in Glacier National Park* (Guilford, CT: Globe Pequot Press, 2005)

National Park Service, *Lake McDonald Lodge Historic District* (Washington, D.C.: National Park Service, 1977)

National Park Service, *Cut Bank Ranger Station Historic District* (Washington, D.C.: National Park Service, 1995)

National Park Service, *East Glacier Ranger Station Historic District* (Washington, D.C.: National Park Service, 1995)

National Park Service, *St. Mary Utility Area Historic District* (Washington, D.C.: National Park Service, 1995)

Ober, M. J., 'The CCC Experience in Glacier National Park', *Montana the Magazine of Western History*, vol. 26 no. 3 (Helena, MT: Montana Historical Society, 1976)

Paige, J. C., *The Civilian Conservation Corps and the National Park Service, 1933-1942 – An Administrative History* (Washington, D.C.: National Park Service, Department of the Interior, 1985)

Redinger, M. A., *The Civilian Conservation Corps as a Tool of the National Park Service: The Development of Glacier and Yellowstone National Parks, 1933-1942* (Missoula, MT: Department of History, University of Montana, 1988)

Rocky Mountains Cooperative Ecosystem Studies Unit, *Glacier National Park Headquarters Historic District Landscape History and Significance Statement* (Santa Fe, NM: National Park Service – Intermountain Region, 2011)

Roosevelt, F. D., *Speech made at Glacier National Park—August 5, 1934* http://www.fdrlibrary.marist.edu/_resources/images/msf/msf00744

Scoyen, E. T., *Glacier National Park Annual Report, Fiscal Year 1933* (West Glacier, MT: Glacier National Park, 1933)

Scoyen, E. T., *Glacier National Park Annual Report, Fiscal Year 1934* (West Glacier, MT: Glacier National Park, 1934)

Scoyen, E. T., *Glacier National Park Annual Report, Fiscal Year 1935* (West Glacier, MT: Glacier National Park, 1935)

Scoyen, E. T., *Glacier National Park Annual Report, Fiscal Year 1936* (West Glacier, MT: Glacier National Park, 1936)

Scoyen, E. T., *Glacier National Park Annual Report, Fiscal Year 1937* (West Glacier, MT: Glacier National Park, 1937)

Scoyen, E. T., *Glacier National Park Annual Report, Fiscal Year 1938* (West Glacier, MT: Glacier National Park, 1938)

Sharp, B., *Civilian Conservation Corps Casualty List for Montana – April, 1933 to August, 1942* (Bozeman, MT: unpublished typescript, 1987)

Sharp, B., *The Civilian Conservation Corps in Montana and under the Fort Missoula C.C.C. District – May, 1933 through July, 1942* (Bozeman, MT: unpublished typescript, 1988)

Shaw, C., *The Flathead Story* (Kalispell, MT: Flathead National Forest, U.S. D.A. Forest Service, 1967)

Smith, M. I., 'Civilian Conservation Corps in Montana: 1933–1942', *The Western Planner*, vol. 37 no. 4, (Cheyenne, WY: Western Planning Resources, Inc., 2016)